DATE DUE			
GAYLORD			PRINTED IN U.S.A.

Civil War Railroads

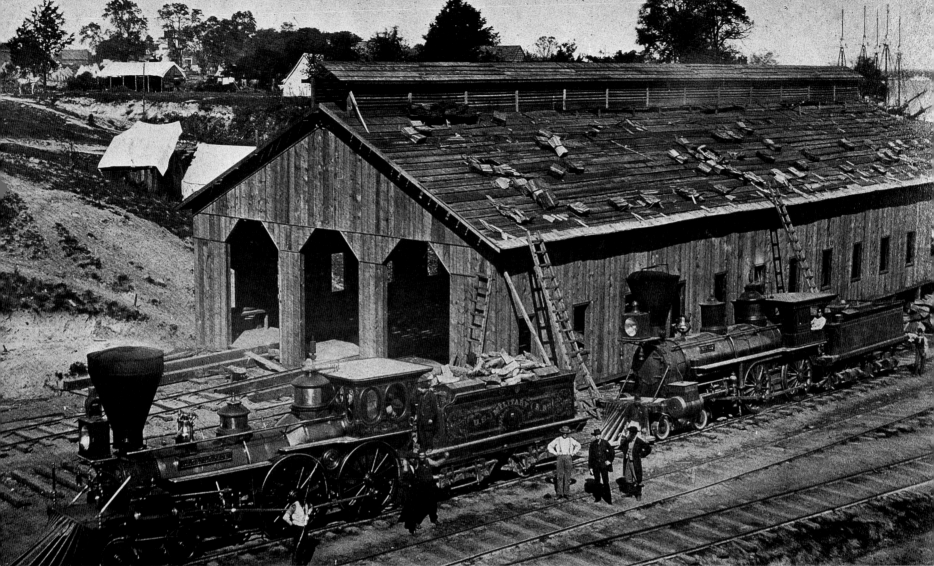

YANKEE RAILROADERS

(Virginia Historical Society photo, Capt. A. J. Russell album,
courtesy of National Archive)

Crews of the United States Military Railroads pose with their iron horses alongside the unfinished enginehouse at City Point, Virginia, September 1st, 1864. The U.S.M.R.R. locomotive at left is the LT. GENL. GRANT, built by Rogers, Ketchum & Grosvenor in 1852, Shop No. 326, as the DELAWARE of the Central Railroad of New Jersey. She was acquired second-hand by U.S.M.R.R. and has been worked over, probably in the Alexandria Shops, with a Mason bell stand and headlight bracket applied and her cylinders rebored, also a new cab applied. The engine behind her is believed to be the Baldwin-built GENL. DIX of th U.S. Military Railroads. Both of these locomotives were in service on the City Point & Army Line.

2

Civil War Railroads

A Pictorial Story of the War Between the States, 1861–1865

GEORGE B. ABDILL

INDIANA UNIVERSITY PRESS

BLOOMINGTON & INDIANAPOLIS

This book is a publication of

Indiana University Press
601 North Morton Street
Bloomington, IN 47404-3797 USA

http://www.indiana.edu/~iupress

Telephone orders   800-842-6796
Fax orders   812-855-7931
E-mail orders   iuporder@indiana.edu

Civil War Railroads, originally published in 1961 by Superior Publishing Company, Seattle, was first reprinted by Indiana University Press in 1999.

The paper used in this publication meets the minimum requirements of American National Standard for Information Sciences—Permanence of Paper for Printed Library Materials, ANSI Z39.48-1984.

Library of Congress Cataloging-in-Publication Data

Abdill, George B.
    Civil War railroads : a pictorial story of the War Between the States, 1861–1865 / George B. Abdill.
        p.   cm.
    ISBN 0-253-33536-1 (alk. paper)
    1. United States—History—Civil War, 1861–1865—Transportation—Pictorial works. 2. Railroads—United States—History—19th century—Pictorial works.   I. Title.
E491.A17   1999
973.7—dc21
                                              98-46924

2 3 4 5   04 03 02 01

Printed in China

Dedicated to those who served
without glory:
The men of the
Military Railway Service

CIVIL WAR RAILROADS

The bloody conflict that swept the United States in 1861 has been known by many names, including the War of Rebellion, the War Between the States, and the generally-accepted Civil War. It could also have been called the Great Railroad War, for the part played by the railroads of both North and South was a vital one, and the final outcome of the strife between brothers was decidedly influenced by the role of the Iron Horse.

The Civil War was the first major military action in which railroads served to any degree, and the commanders in many instances were slow to grasp the great possibilities offered by the comparatively new mode of transport. When the progressive leaders began to utilize the rails for transport of troops, supplies, wounded, and the other impedimentia of warfare, the advantages soon became apparent; as a result, the rail lines became military targets of prime importance and the tide of battle was often turned by the ability of the railroads to rush up reinforcements and keep up a steady flow of ammunition, rations, and forage.

The Confederate Government's defeat was due, in a large measure, to the lack of a concentrated authority to seize and operate the railroads in the South. Attempts were made to bring about a united effort of the various roads existing in the South, but the precept of Government seizure and control of the railways as a military necessity was contrary to the theory of State's Rights, and the war effort was constantly hampered by this obstruction.

The magic of the camera has left us a wealth of photographs depicting the struggle between North and South during the Civil War, captured by such intrepid artists as Mathew Brady, Capt.

A. J. Russell, Alexander Gardner, T. H. O'Sullivan, Geo. N. Barnard, John Reekie, David Knox, James Gardner, Sam A. Cooley, S. R. Seibert, Thomas C. Roche, George S. Cook, Andrew Lytle, J. F. Coonley, Wood & Gibson, and others.

From the collections of the National Archives, the Library of Congress, the Smithsonian Institution, the Ansco Corporation, and a number of private collectors, the author has assembled a photographic record of the Iron Horse at war. The pictures present a graphic story of our American railroads and the men who ran them, starting with John Brown's raid on Harper's Ferry and following through the bloody years to the peace at Appomattox. The history of the terrible conflict has filled volumes, but this album attempts to detail the neglected story of those brave men, Confederate and Union alike, who defended their faith while serving on the iron trails leading to battle.

The author has attempted to be completely impartial in recounting the stories in this volume, and with good reason. One great-grandfather, Samuel Creson, served the Confederate flag with a Kentucky cavalry outfit; born in North Carolina, he had married Nancy Adeline Hutchins, a descendant of a pioneer Virginia family that settled on the James River below Richmond in 1610. Although her family held slaves during their early years in the Colony, their Quaker religion had moved them to liberate their Negroes by Deeds of Manumission long before the storm clouds of the Civil War began to gather. Two other great-grandfathers served in the Civil War on the side of the North; George B. Abdill was a member of Capt. James Finican's Company "C", 65th Illinois Volunteer Infantry, known as the "Scotch Regiment" and under the command of Colonel William S. Stewart; Adelmer Price, a maternal ancestor, was a member of "K" Company, 3rd Minnesota Cavalry, and spent the War years combating the Sioux Indians during their uprising in Minnesota.

If the photos seem predominately Northern, it must be explained that extremely few Confederate photographers left any existing pictures of the railroads of the South.

The battlefields of the War proved to be great training ground for railroad builders, and men who had crossed sabers or levelled muskets at one another were to find themselves shoulder to shoulder, repelling Indian attacks while driving the steel of the transcontinental railroads across the plains of the West.

The writer hopes that the pictures and stories bring enjoyment to the reader, along with a better understanding of the problems of railroaders at war; he served as a locomotive engineer in "C" Company, 744th Railway Operating Battalion, during World War II, running his engine in France, Belgium, and Germany, and has a first-hand knowledge of railroading under fire.

GEORGE B. ABDILL
Roseburg, Oregon

ACKNOWLEDGEMENTS

The search for photographs and reference material for this volume extended from the Pacific to the Atlantic and from Canada to the Gulf; the list of those who assisted in the compilation of the book is indeed long.

The whole-hearted cooperation of Mr. Forest L. Williams, Archivist in Charge of the Still Picture Branch, National Archives, Washington, D.C., has made the volume possible through his efforts in bringing to light the rare old photographs of Civil War railroads.

Special thanks are also due to Mr. Raymond B. Carneal, Durham, North Carolina. Mr. Carneal's collection of data on railroads of the South is probably the most complete record ever assembled, and he has labored under physical pain and afflictions almost beyond endurance to generously supply information for this work.

Others who have aided in various ways are: Miss Josephine Cobb and Mr. Victor Gondos, Jr., National Archives & Records Service; Mr. Hirst D. Milhollen and Mr. Donald C. Holmes, Library of Congress; Mr. Philip M. Mikoda, Ansco Corporation; Mr. L. W. Sagle, Baltimore & Ohio Railroad; Mr. Chas. E. Fisher, Railway & Locomotive Historical Society; Mr. John H. White, Jr., Smithsonian Institution; Mr. Beaumont Newhall, George Eastman House; Mr. J. G. Shea, Southern Pacific Company; Mr. Lee Borah, Mr. James N. Sites, and Mr. Harry Eddy, Association of American Railroads; Lt. Col. Thomas B. Clagett, Hdqs., Department of the Army; Lt. Col. Floyd L. Francisco and Col. B. E. Kendall, Office of the Quartermaster General, Washington, D.C.; Col. Robert S. Henry, Alexandria, Virginia; Mr. Charles R. Dunlap, Pennsylvania Railroad; Mr. Harry E. Hammer, Reading Railroad; Mr. C. E. Mervine, Jr., Richmond, Fredericksburg & Potomac Railroad; Mr. Donald T. Martin, Atlantic Coast Line Railroad; Mr. Ronald L. Coleman, Central of Georgia Railway; Mr. Julian L. James and Mr. Edison H. Thomas, Louisville & Nashville Railroad; Mr. Kenneth Hood, Norfolk & Western Railway; Mr. B. E. Young, Southern Railway; Mr. H. L. Broadbelt, owner of the noted Baldwin Loco. Works negative collection, Hershey, Pennsylvania; Mr. L. W. Rice, Silver Spring, Maryland; Mr. H. L. Goldsmith, Woodside, New York; Mrs. Ralph Catterall, Valentine Museum, Richmond, Va.; Mr. John M. Jennings, Virginia Historical Society, Richmond, Va.; and others.

The writer is indebted to Mr. Thomas Norrell, Silver Spring, Maryland, for his generous aid in supplying photographs and information regarding the railroads of the Civil War.

Thanks are also due Miss Carol Trimble, Mrs. Ruth Hansen, Miss Muriel Mitchell, and the staff of the Douglas County Library, Roseburg, Oregon, who have spared no efforts in assisting in the quest for valuable research material. Mr. Art French, Mr. Jay Golden, and Mr. Bob Leber of the Photo Lab, Roseburg, Oregon, have aided greatly in reproducing the old prints in the book. Mr. Laymond E. "Jeff" Davis, Southern Pacific switchman of Roseburg and a native son of Tennessee, deserves mention for his help regarding the region around Chattanooga and the South in general.

Publisher Albert P. Salisbury must be commended for his willingness to produce the book in album format, designed to display the photographs to the best possible advantage.

And lastly, a fanfare of trumpets for my patient and loving wife. Her encouragement and patient understanding as the Civil War was re-fought in our home has made my dream of this book a reality.

JOHN BROWN'S BODY

The first blood shed by railroaders in the struggle over the slavery question flowed at Harper's Ferry on October 17, 1859. John Brown, the bearded old Abolitionist, raided the quiet village shown here at the junction of the Shenandoah with the Potomac River and captured the Federal Arsenal located there. The eastbound night express train of the Baltimore & Ohio Railroad was stopped by Brown's raiders and forbidden to pass. In the skirmishing during the raid, Station Master Fontaine Beckham and the station porter, Hayward Sheppard, both were mortally wounded. Engineer William McKay and Conductor A. J. Phelps backed the night express train away from the station while the fighting was in progress, and shortly after daylight the raiders permitted them to proceed on their run toward Baltimore. The shooting of Beckham and Sheppard and the capture and delay of the express was a foretaste of the bloody actions that would center around the railroads in the dark days of the Civil War that lay ahead.

The Baltimore & Ohio Railroad, chartered in 1827, had started construction in 1828 and the rails had reached Harper's Ferry on December 1, 1834; the road was extended to Cumberland in 1842 and was completed into Wheeling on January 1, 1853.

Harper's Ferry was the junction of the Baltimore & Ohio with the Winchester & Potomac Railroad, a short line chartered in 1830 and opened from Winchester, Virginia, to Harper's Ferry in 1836. When the War began, the 32-mile road had two locomotives, both of which were taken over by the U.S. Military Railroad; one of these, a 4-4-0 built by Eastwick & Harrison in 1841, became the PRESIDENT on the USMRR roster, and the other, a Norris product, bore the name, ANCIENT.

RAILS GO TO WAR

The Federal Government, in an act dated January 31, 1862, set up the machinery for an agency to control the operations of captured Southern railroads, and on February 11th of 1862, Daniel C. McCallum was appointed military director and superintendent of railroads in the United States, cloaked with authority to take possession of railroads, rolling stock, and equipment and to operate such lines required for the transport of troops, arms, ammunition, and military supplies. By this action, the foundation was laid for the United States Military Railroads, the forerunner of our present Military Railway Service.

Prior to the establishment of the Military Railroads, the control of the lines operated in war zones had been vested in the Department of the Army in charge of the affected area. As an example of this, General Sherman had appointed John B. Anderson as railroad director for the Department of the Ohio in November of 1861. By an act of Congress approved in 1864, the Quartermaster Department was given charge of railroads, and several roads in the West were operated under control of the QM Department, including the Memphis & Little Rock and the New Orleans, Opelousas & Great Western.

In addition to establishing Government control over captured lines, the act of January 31, 1862, gave the Government the authority to order the nation's railroads to transport troops and the necessities of war to the exclusion of all other business.

Included in the railway equipment purchased by the Government for use on the Military Railroads was the wood-burner GENL. HAUPT, an American type locomotive built by Wm. Mason in 1863.

Although the officers of the United States Military Railroads carried military titles, the operating personnel were hired civilians, hence the civilian garb on the train and engine crew posing here with their war horse.

DRIVING FORCE

(Courtesy of the Library of Congress)

Credit for much of the initial groundwork and efficiency of the Military Railroads and the Construction Corps must go to the shrewd engineer pictured here. Herman Haupt was born in Pennsylvania in 1817 and graduated from West Point at the age of 18, along with George Meade, in the Class of 1835. Haupt resigned his commission shortly after graduation and began a career of railroad construction, starting on the Western Maryland Railroad. He was later appointed Professor of Mathematics and Engineering at Pennsylvania College, Gettysburg, and while in that position he attracted the attention of J. Edgar Thomson, Chief Engineer of the Pennsylvania Railroad. Haupt left his college teaching to serve as Thomson's assistant, and soon rose to the position of General Superintendent of the Pennsylvania Railroad, and became Chief Engi-

neer of that line in 1853. In 1856 he resigned and took charge of construction of the famous Hoosac Tunnel on the Troy & Greenfield Railroad in Massachusetts.

Haupt's reputation as an engineer was well-known, and in early 1862 he was summoned to Washington by Secretary of War Stanton to aid in reconstruction and operation of the rail lines serving the Army of the Potomac in northern Virginia. His first task was to restore a portion of the damaged road from Aquia Creek toward Fredericksburg, and he was employed in a civilian capacity. He was soon made a colonel on the staff of General McDowell, a friend from the old academy days at West Point, and commenced building up a construction corps. Soldiers were at first detailed for this work, but Haupt preferred civilians and was instrumental in their future use on the Military Railroad projects.

Haupt was commissioned a brigadier general of volunteers on September 5th, 1862. He served under a parade of Union commanders, including McDowell, Pope, McClellan, Burnside, Hooker, and Meade. His quarrels with regular Army officers are related elsewhere in this volume. General D. C. McCallum was nominally his superior in the transportation forces, but the two men worked together amiably, McCallum in the office and Haupt in the field. Haupt refused to accept the comission offered him, preferring to remain in charge of railway construction as a civilian; this led to an angry exchange with Secretary Stanton, and Haupt was relieved on September 14, 1863. The value of his services in organizing the Construction Corps of the Military Railroads was priceless, and they contributed greatly to all future successes of that arm of the service. After the war Haupt served with the Richmond & Danville Railroad, then helped complete the transcontinental Northern Pacific. He later served with a company that completed a pipeline from the Allegheny Valley to tidewater, fighting the opposition of powerful rail lines and rival oil companies. He authored two books, "The General Theory of Bridge Construction," published in 1851, and "Reminiscences," privately published in 1901.

Death came to the courageous veteran on December 14, 1905. He was aboard a Pennsylvania Railroad passenger train bound for Washington when a sudden heart attack ended his turbulent career, quite fittingly amid the railroad surroundings he had loved and fought for so gallantly.

CANNY SCOT

Daniel Craig McCallum was born in Scotland in 1815 and migrated to the United States with his parents in the 1820's. Young Dan McCallum grew up in Rochester, New York, and after his elementary schooling he entered the employ of the New York & Erie Railroad. He studied engineering and architecture, and his administrative talents won him steady promotion. He rose to the position of superintendent of the road's Susquehanna Division and in 1854 was appointed General Superintendent of the New York & Erie lines. In 1859 he designed and patented a railroad bridge called an Inflexible Arched Truss Bridge, and when the Civil War broke out in 1861, he was president of the McCallum Bridge Company, a concern that specialized in railway bridges. A large and powerful man, McCallum had gained a reputation of being strict with his railroad employees, and ruled his Division with iron discipline.

On February 11, 1862, an order from Secretary of War Edwin M. Stanton appointed McCallum as military director and superintendent of railroads in the United States. Commissioned a colonel, the genial McCallum later rose to the rank of a major general. He had sweeping power to take over any railroad or railroad equipment needed to transport troops or military supplies, but managed to operate the necessary lines with but little friction. His major problem was to prevent various Union officers from interfering with his trains and telegraph lines, and to force commanders to unload and release empty cars that were badly needed.

McCallum succeeded John B. Anderson as general manager of the military railroads in the West, and it was in this theater that he achieved some of his best results in organization and efficient railroad operation.

The reports of Brevet Brigadier General D. C. McCallum, Director & General Manager of the Military Railroads of the United States, rendered May 26th, 1866, are an invaluable source of information regarding the railroads in the Civil War, and much of the information in this book is drawn from that source.

McCallum's talents were not limited to railroading; he designed St. Joseph's Church in Rochester, New York, and had a book of his own verse published under the title, THE WATER MILL. The strain of the war years had taken a heavy

(Courtesy of National Archive)

toll and McCallum's rugged physique was sapped by illness. He passed away in 1878 at the age of 63 and the history of his great contributions toward the final victory of the Union forces is buried in the forgotten records of that bloody struggle.

IN JOHNNY REB'S WAKE

This view shows the remains of the railroad facilities at Manassas Junction, Virginia, after the point had been evacuated by Confederate troops in March of 1862. Alexander Gardner, the noted Civil War photographer, reported that the Confederate troops burned a bridge south of the Junction, thinking all the rolling stock had been withdrawn. This burned bridge marooned two trains, which the Rebels fired to prevent them from falling into Union hands. Only 6 cars escaped the flames; these were loaded with flour and the camp equipment of a South Carolina brigade. Also destroyed was the railroad depot, machine shop, and repair shops.

Manassas Junction was located at the juncture of the Orange & Alexandria Railroad and the Manassas Gap Railroad, about halfway between Alexandria and Warrenton Junction, Virginia. The Manassas Gap Railroad ran westerly from this point to Strasburg and Mt. Jackson, Virginia. The Junction was about 27 miles south of Alexandria, and about 62 miles east of Strasburg. General Haupt repaired the Gap Road from Rectortown to Piedmont in 1862 in support of General McDowell's forces, who were attempting to catch "Stonewall" Jackson's forces in the Shenandoah Valley. After repairing 5 bridges across Goose Creek, destroyed by the Confederates, Haupt received word of a bad break in the line near the summit. He took his crew to the scene, arriving shortly after daybreak on Sunday, June 1st, 1862. Rebels or guerrillas had loosened the brakes on a dozen or more cars at the summit siding and started them rolling down a steep grade, after having removed a number of ties and rails from the main line at a point some distance down the mountain. The runaway cars hit the gap and piled up in jumbled heap of ruins.

Haupt divided his labor group into two parties and set them to work at each end of the break in the track. The broken cars were tumbled down the steep hillside, and the ties and rails that had been thrown down the high bank by the train wreckers were hauled back up to the roadbed and put in place. One of McDowell's engineer officers who had viewed the wreck had advised McDowell that it would require at least two days to repair the damage. General Haupt rode a locomotive over the repaired site before 10:00 A.M. of the day he had started reconstruction, and steamed on into Front Royal, much to the surprise of General McDowell.

General Geary's command patrolled the Manassas Gap road to protect it, but operations were complicated by Army officers who commandeered the telegraph line used for train movements. Haupt reported it was once necessary for him to walk eight miles in an attempt to move a train. No timetable had been put in effect and the loaded trains moving to Front Royal had rights over opposing empties; the empty trains were compelled to return with a flagman walking in advance and to yield the right of way to any trains met.

———•———

GAP ROAD RUINS

This photo shows the remains of burned cars and the turntable at Manassas Junction in 1862. The locomotive which appears in both photos of the Junction is probably one of the Denmead & Son engines belonging to the Manassas Gap Railroad; the line owned 9 locomotives, all but one of which were built by Denmead & Son in their factory in Baltimore, Maryland.

(Courtesy of the Southern Railway)

VIRGINA RAIL CENTER

The Orange & Alexandria Railroad was chartered in 1848 and built a standard gauge line from Alexandria southwesterly across Virginia to Gordonsville. In 1859 the road was placed in operation to Lynchburg, 170 miles south of Alexandria; the section between Gordonsville and Charlottesville was owned by the Virginia Central Railroad and the Orange & Alexandria used that road's rails between the two points to reach its' own southern extension from Charlottesville to Lynchburg, where it met the 5 foot gauge Virginia & Tennessee Railroad, connecting Virginia with Tennessee and northern Georgia and Alabama.

When the Civil War broke out, the Orange & Alexandria was in a very exposed position and President John S. Barbour, Jr., organized a force of guards to protect the line. Most of the 16 engines in use on the road, along with a majority of the rolling stock, were moved south of Manassas Junction to

14

keep them out of Federal hands. Barbour, a former United States Congressman and scion of a prominent Old Dominion family, was a man of great energy and resolve. When Confederate forces captured seven U.S. Military Railroad engines in the Second Manassas battle, Barbour and about 30 employees managed to get them across the bridgeless waters of the Rappahannock and moved them behind the Confederate lines.

The ebb and flow of battle swept across the Orange & Alexandria and the Union Army used portions of it to their advantage. This photo shows the big covered brick roundhouse in Alexandria while it was in the hands of the Union troops. The engine in the foreground is the United States Military Railroad's LION, a 4-4-0 built by the New Jersey Locomotive & Machine Company in 1862. Note her odd oval-shaped windows in the front and side of the cab. Partly hidden behind the LION is another United States Military R.R. locomotive, the HUMMING BIRD. This 4-4-0 was built by Baldwin in 1855 for the Philadelphia & Reading Railway and was acquired from that line by the Federal Government. She bore Baldwin's Shop No. 633, had 16x22 inch cylinders and 60 inch driving wheels. The third locomotive, standing in the distance, has not been identified.

Note the discarded wooden locomotive cab and stave pilots in the scrap pile in the right foreground. This eastern view of the roundhouse and yards was reportedly taken in 1863.

DISRUPTED PASSAGE

This view taken by Timothy H. O'Sullivan in October of 1863 shows the line of the Orange & Alexandria Railroad between Bristow Station and the Rappahannock River. Confederates have destroyed the track by heating the rails over burning piles of ties. The tangle of telegraph wire in the foreground bears mute witness to the fate of the lines of communication.
(Courtesy of the Library of Congress)

BULL RUN CROSSING

In April of 1863 the Military Railroad reopened the line of the Orange & Alexandria R.R. south to Bealeton and used it for a short time to supply a Federal force on the Rappahannock. In June the entire line was evacuated and the equipment withdrawn to Alexandria and Washington. Repairs were begun in July and the road was opened to Culpeper to supply General Meade's army. General Haupt reported that guerrilla action increased after the battle of Chancellorsville, necessitating 30 to 50 men being used to guard each train.

One one occasion a Military Railroad train steaming through the Virginia countryside came upon one of the wooden bridges of the line that had been fired by a party of guerrillas or raiders. The bridge was burning in its mid-section and at both ends, and five men who had fired it made their escape on horseback as the train approached. In addition to burning bridges, the enemy harrassed the Army railroaders by placing obstructions on the track and by firing on the trains running on the road.

The O. & A. was abandoned by the Federals in October of 1863 south of Bull Run and thoroughly destroyed by the Confederates from Manassas Junction nearly to Brandy Station. It was repaired to Culpeper in November of 1863 and used through the winter, then abandoned back to Burke's Station in May of 1864; the road was reopened to the Rappahannock in the fall of 1864, then abandoned back to Manassas and operated to that point until Nov. 10th, 1864, then abandoned back to Fairfax, 16 miles from Alexandria, and that portion was operated until the close of the war. On June 27th, 1865, the Orange & Alexandria was returned to the Board of Public Works of Virginia; the line is now part of the main stem of the Southern Railway System.

This photo shows a Military Railroad train on the rebuilt Bull Run bridge with a motley consist, including box cars, flat cars, and two old wooden Pennsylvania Railroad coaches. The Union troopers in the immediate foreground may be part of the guard force used to protect the railroad bridge from enemy and guerrilla action.

NATURAL COVER

This photo, probably taken by Capt. A. J. Russell, bore the caption: "View on Pope's Head, Near Burnt Bridge, Orange & Alexandria Railroad." The dense stand of brush and timber afforded an effective screen to hide the Rebel and guerrilla snipers and raiding parties intent on damaging the operations of the U.S. Military Railroads.

(Virginia Historical Society photo, courtesy of National Archives)

(Courtesy of the National Archives)

PENINSULAR CAMPAIGN

Early in March of 1862, in preparation for his campaign in the Peninsula of Virginia, General McClellan ordered General D. C. McCallum to have 5 locomotives and 80 cars loaded on vessels in the Baltimore harbor ready to move out whenever ordered. The equipment was purchased second-hand from various Northern railroads, loaded as directed, and early in May of 1862 the flotilla was sent steaming south to White House, Virginia, where it was placed upon the Richmond & York River Railroad, a 38-mile standard gauge road running from Richmond to West Point, Virginia. A sixth locomotive was sent to the road in June and toward the end of that month the Military Railroad's trains were running to within about four miles of Richmond. One stirring incident took place on the line at Tunstall's Station, which was captured by a force of Confederate cavalry. They cut the telegraph wire and felled a tree across the tracks, but the engineer on an approaching Union troop train spied the obstruction and sent his engine forward with a wide-open throttle. The locomotive hit the tree and tossed it clear, allowing the train to escape, although rebel gunfire killed and wounded some of the troops on it.

When McClellan withdrew his operations to the James River in late June, the Pamunkey River bridge was destroyed and the six locomotives and the rolling stock damaged and left behind. The engines EXETER, SPARK, SPEEDWELL, ONTARIO, and WYANDANK were taken by the Confederates but recovered and sold in 1865; no record exists for the sixth engine, the LINCOLN, after 1862 so she was possibly destroyed at the time of the evacuation. This view is reputed to show the White House Landing on the Pamunkey, with a locomotive of the U.S. Military Railroad loaded on a vessel and visible over the bridge; in the left foreground is the portable dark-room of the photographer who exposed this plate.

CAR SHORTAGE

This view shows the remains of a string of railroad cars burned by raiders in northern Virginia. When General Pope was driven back along the Orange & Alexandria Railroad in the latter part of August, 1862, the Military Railroad lost 295 cars to the advancing Confederates.

In addition to the dangers of operating in a war zone subject to attack by troops or guerrillas, the Army railroaders encountered the same problems that were to plague their civilian brethren for many years to come. The time book of a Military Railroad conductor, now in possession of Mr. Chas. E. Fisher of the Railway & Locomotive Historical Society, cites an instance of the danger of encountering loose livestock. At 8:25 P.M. on the date of this incident, the locomotive ran over two cows that had strayed onto the track; the cows were both killed, the engine damaged on one side, and eight cars of the train were derailed. The crew patched up the engine and ran on into the Alexandria terminal where the wreck was reported. They then coupled onto the wrecking outfit stationed there and returned to the derailed train. The work of getting the cars back on the track must have proceeded smoothly, for the crew had them back on the iron and chuffed back into Alexandria at 1:15 A.M.

In a day when derailments were commonplace, the railroaders were adept at coaxing the wheels back onto the rails, and work of this nature was often done with the aid of sticks of wood from the locomotive's fuel supply, the blocks being used in the same manner in which metal frogs are now used.

(Courtesy of Library of Congress)

TROOP MOVEMENT

This scene shows the yards and roundhouse of the Orange & Alexandria Railroad at Alexandria, Virginia; the Union soldiers lining the tracks and platform are reportedly part of McClellan's forces who were belatedly ordered to the aid of General John Pope in the bitter campaign in the fall of 1862. Herman Haupt's telegraph operators had kept him advised of conditions at the front and the former West Pointer probably had more knowledge of the needs of the Army than any other individual. Haupt was instructed to locate General McClellan for consultation, the order coming from General Halleck. The railroader procured a row-boat and searched for "Little Mac," finding him with his staff in the cabin of a steamer on the Potomac some distance below Alexandria. McClellan would not authorize Haupt's proposal to load troops to move toward Bull Run, but Haupt procured some train guards from General Hancock and his crews succeeded in bringing off a large number of the wounded from around Fairfax Station.

Haupt's constant struggle against interference by Army

brass is well illustrated by the Sturgis affair. Four trains loaded with wounded were hours overdue at Alexandria, and Haupt was burning the midnight oil in anxiety over their delay. Soon one of his conductors, lantern in hand, came striding out of the dark to inform him that the trains had been halted about four miles out of town by order of General Sturgis, who desired the equipment to move his command. Haupt and Supt. Devereux went to Sturgis' camp to explain that the trains must be released and run to the terminal for unloading and servicing of the engines before they could return south. When Haupt told Sturgis that the delay was endangering General Pope's forces, the tipsy Sturgis exclaimed: "I don't care for John Pope a pinch of owl dung!" Sturgis further exposed his lack of railroad knowledge by ordering the engines of the four trains he was holding to cut off and run to Alexandria for wood and water; this while the trains were standing one behind the other on a single track with no siding nearby to permit them to saw by each other! While at Sturgis' head-

20

quarters, Haupt received a message from Gen. Halleck stating that if Sturgis interfered with the railroad, Halleck would arrest him. When Sturgis' Chief of Staff finally impressed the contents of this message upon him, stressing that Halleck proposed to arrest him, Sturgis replied: "He does, does he? Well, then, take your damned railroad!"

IRON WARHORSE

This photograph taken at the water tanks at City Point, Virginia, presents a good broadside view of one of the 4-4-0 type woodburners built by R. Norris & Son for use on the U.S. Military Railroads; the engine may be the GOVERNOR NYE. Behind the water tank at left is the spur track leading out on a trestle to the Magazine Wharf, where munitions for Grant's army was unloaded for transferral to the freight cars.

It was probably on such a locomotive as the one pictured here that a Union force made a foray into Virginia's "No Man's Land" in search of General George B. McClellan. Communications were frequently disrupted, especially in the earlier days of the War, and segments of the armies often lost direct contact with each other. General Rufus Ingalls came to Herman Haupt and requested that he be taken to Rectortown on the Manassas Gap Railroad, as Ingalls had received information that General McClellan had moved to that point and established a headquarters there. Haupt did not believe this rumor, but Ingalls insisted and a trip was arranged. Haupt rounded up a crew and coupled two flat cars behind an engine; a detail of soldier-guards were loaded on these flat cars and the special chuffed off down the Gap Road. The line passed through territory known to be frequented by Confederate forces and had not been used for some time. Tall grass hid the rails and caused the woodburner to slip badly, soon exhausting the supply of sand. One of the flat cars was uncoupled and left behind to lighten the load, but the engine, sand dome empty, continued to slip and spin her drivers on the grassy rail. The condition became so bad that on some of the grades the troopers had to trot ahead and place small pebbles of ballast on the rail to be crushed by the pony trucks in order to provide traction for the driving wheels. The situation grew so bad that the remaining flat car was left behind, the guards being taken aboard the locomotive. When the water in the tender ran low, the men formed a bucket brigade and refilled the tank from trackside streams.

It was a clear, quiet day and Haupt feared that the unusual activity on the deserted Manassas Gap Railroad would attract the unwanted attention of roving troopers of the Confederacy. The noise created by the engine as she lost her footing on the slippery rails could be heard for a long distance, and her billow of white exhaust hung over the expedition like a giant marker. Flanges squealed on the rusty iron as the little kettle rounded the curves, the men aboard her keeping a keen watch for the approach of Rebel cavalrymen. Darkness fell and the train crept on, reaching Rectortown after midnight. No trace of McClellan could be found and the locomotive cautiously was backed to Manassas Junction and returned to the safety of the Union lines at Fairfax.

(Courtesy of the Library of Congress)

UNION MILLS STATION

This station and siding on the Orange & Alexandria Railroad (now Clifton, Virginia) was the scene of much activity during the Civil War. The photo shows two locomotives and cars on the main line, while other cars loaded with wheels and rails stand on the side track opposite the two wooden water tanks; Union pickets shoulder their muskets as they stand guard duty on the rim of the bank at the right.

In August of 1862, the main line near Union Mills was tied up at a critical time when the U.S. Military Railroad engine SECRETARY ran into the rear end of another train, obstructing the main line of supply to the Union front. Haupt ordered out wrecking and construction trains and the work of clearing the wreck was pushed rapidly, under the threat of an attack at any moment by Confederate forces.

On September 1st, 1862, the rebels were reported at or near Fairfax Courthouse and the Union troops at Fairfax Station under command of Major Haller retreated toward Alexandria, leaving Haupt's railroad crews in a very exposed position. He sent instruction to the agent, McCrickett, at Fairfax to load all the supplies he could, pile the wounded on top of the cars, and evacuate that point. McCrickett was further instructed to burn any forage and supplies he could not move, then to escape on foot; Haupt's message to him read, in part: "Keep cool and trust your legs and the bushes for escape." The gallant McCrickett, later to lose his life in a train wreck, sent a message to Supt. Devereux acknowledging the Haupt order, saying: "All right. I feel perfectly cool and wet; have been fording streams and wading ditches since 4 A.M."

Reported to have been the last man to leave the bloody field of Second Bull Run, or Manassas, McCrickett sent the following final message from Fairfax Station on September 2, 1862.

J. H. Devereux:
    Have fired it. Good-by.
                                    McC.

GUARDIANS OF THE IRON ROAD

This photo, reportedly taken on the Orange & Alexandria Railroad, shows a group of Union troops assigned to guard the road against rebel raiders and guerrillas; in the background is a railway trestle, water tanks and pumping station, and a partly-completed blockhouse. The necessity for these guards is evidenced in the following message:

Alexandria Depot, July 26, 1863.

General Herman Haupt:

No. 1 train this A.M. found, when a mile and a half east of Burkes, a rail taken out of the track and horseshoes on rail. Engine was reversed and brakes put hard down. Engine jumped the break and, with two cars, passed on. Had it been rail on opposite side, the whole train would have run off the track down a twelve-foot bank. Before train was checked twelve rebels in grey and blue coats and pants, and all with guns, pushed out of the bushes, whilst the guard of the Fourth Delaware then took a hand and, after a few shots, jumped off the train and had a foot-race through the woods after the rebels. One fat rebel particularly distinguished himself in getting out of sight. The guard saved the train and its convoy, and Providence saved a smash-up which, for some time, would have prevented the Army of the Potomac from receiving supplies.

It is pitiful that a handful of rebels can be allowed the chance of so retarding the progress of our army in such measure as an accident like this might cause. I earnestly ask that 200 men be at once stationed from Accotink to Burkes. . . .

J. H. Devereux.

This message came from the Military Railroad superintendent at Alexandria, and resulted in a report of the incident from General Haupt to General Rufus Ingalls, requesting cavalry patrols and other security measurers to protect the trains from such incidents, which Haupt stated were daily occurrences.

(Courtesy of the National Archives)

(Courtesy of the Library of Congress)

BATTERED RAMPARTS

Harper's Ferry, with the vital arsenal located near the Baltimore & Ohio Railroad's main line to the west, was one of the first targets of the Confederacy. On April 18, 1861, just six days after the first shells burst over Fort Sumter, Capt. John D. Imboden of the Staunton Artillery led a force of Virginia militia, including the Monticello Guards and the Albemarle Rifles, on a rail expedition along the Orange & Alexandria and the Manassas Gap railroads, headed for the Federal arsenal at Harper's Ferry. The troops occupied the town and it was soon placed under the command of Thomas J. Jackson; the arsenal was put to work turning out Harper's Ferry muskets for the Confederate army. When a Union advance threatened Jackson's garrison in June of 1861, he laid waste the B&O main line from Point of Rocks to Martinsburg, a distance of 54 miles; the big shops at Martinsburg were damaged, over 40 locomotives and more than 380 cars destroyed, and 23 bridges burned. The big B&O bridge over the Potomac at Harper's Ferry was blown up, with the results shown here, and the main line was tied up until March 28, 1862.

The railroad bridge at this site was destroyed and rebuilt nine times during the war, one of the temporary trestle bridges being washed away, along with a number of loaded coal cars spotted on it in an effort to hold the trestle in place during the freshet.

24

The B&O suffered many losses during the War, including some damage caused by Union troops; on one occasion their cooking fires got out of control and burned 23 cars loaded with hay. In April of 1863, Confederates led by Imboden and Jones destroyed a number of bridges, including the largest iron bridge on the road, a structure that spanned the Monongahela River. Jubal Early hit the line in the summer of 1864, doing so much damage that the road was not open for through traffic until September, when Sheridan defeated Early's troops at the battle of Winchester.

In the immediate foreground of this photograph, reproduced from a damaged glass plate, can be seen the debris-filled dry bed of the old Chesapeake & Ohio canal.

———•———

ONE MORE RIVER

These smouldering ruins mark the remains of the railroad bridge over the North Anna River on the line of the Richmond, Fredericksburg & Potomac Railroad. When the War came to this Virginia line and the Federals moved against Fredericksburg in 1862, the Confederates burned the Rappahannock River bridge there. For the duration of the conflict, the northern terminus of the line operated out of Richmond under the Stars and Bars was located at Hamilton's Crossing, about four miles south of Fredericksburg. Yankee raiders hit the road in May of 1862, wiping out the South Anna bridge and cutting the service north of that point for nearly five months. Again in May of 1864, Sheridan's troopers moving from Spotsylvania Courthouse hit the RF&P, burning both the North Anna and South Anna bridges and wrecking five miles of the road. In March of 1865, Union forces wiped out the four main bridges on the Rebel-held section of the line and put the torch to a 28-car freight train. When the War began, the RF&P had 10 eight-wheeled engines; these were named the JNO. A. LANCASTER; GEO. W. MUNFORD; THOMAS SHARP; JAMES BOSHER; NORTH STAR; ECLIPSE; G. A. MYERS; NICH. MILLS; TECUMSEH; and HENRY CLAY. The line also had the G. P. R. JAMES, a four-wheeled locomotive; 88 slaves; and a dark bay horse.

(Courtesy of the National Archives)

BORDER ROAD

The Baltimore & Ohio Railroad's main line from Baltimore to Wheeling and Parkersburg, on the Ohio River, was located in an exposed position and was subjected to damage from both Confederate and Union forces during the Civil War. In May of 1861 about 100 miles of the B&O main stem was occupied by Confederates, who controlled the road from Point of Rocks on the east to Cumberland on the west. The troops commanded by T. J. "Stonewall" Jackson permitted the B&O trains to run over this segment and the road found itself in the unusual position of operating through the lines of two opposing armies.

W. P. Smith, Master of Transportation for the B&O, kept a diary in which he recorded some of the stirring events that took place on the road during the War years. Early in June of 1861 a bridge on the road was destroyed and a train of about 50 cars of coal went hurtling to destruction in a deep ravine. This wreckage took fire and burned for several month, the heat being so great that the metal trucks of the old "pot" type coal hoppers were melted.

When rebel forces under General Robert E. Lee invaded Maryland in the fall of 1862, the big B&O suspension bridge at Monocacy was blown up. Raids and rumors of raids kept the B&O Operating Department constantly stirred up, and the road experimented with armored trains in an effort to protect its property. These ironclad trains presented a formidable target and the enemy was very reluctant to attack these fortresses on wheels, although on one occasion they succeeded in capturing an armored train and burned the cars, after having disabled the locomotive by an artillery shell which pierced the boiler.

This view of a Baltimore & Ohio train was taken in June of 1858 and shows an artists' excursion crossing the Alleghenies behind a funnel-stacked eightwheeler; the train has halted for the photographer on one of the famous truss bridges designed by Wendel Bollman.

----------●----------

SOMEWHERE IN VIRGINIA
The only identification connected with this photo is that the scene reportedly was taken on the Orange & Alexandria Railroad in 1862. The engine probably belongs to the O&A, although a possibility exists that she may have been one of the older locomotives purchased from other lines by the U.S. Military Railroad.

Many interesting stories of Virginia railroading appeared in a series of articles written for "Locomotive Engineering" in the 1890's by Carter S. Anderson, a conductor on the Virginia Central; these were titled: "Train Running For The Confederacy" and present a very human side of military railroading in time of war. Anderson, who spent his last years as Storekeeper for the Chesapeake & Ohio in Richmond, recalled that a great many of the Confederate railroaders drank whiskey; when a number of Virginia Central crews were collected for a heavy troop movement at Charlottesville, Supt. Whitcomb stated he would: ". . . be glad to have one sober man in each crew and think it best not to put all the whisky men together." Anderson's engineer during this troop movement was John Whalley, in charge of the locomotive MONROE; the fireman was a gingerbread-colored Negro named John Wesley. Engineer Whalley was a big man, extremely good-natured, but a hard drinker and inclined to be surly when in his cups. When the convoy of troop trains was ready to move, Conductor Anderson discovered that Engineer Whalley and the free

Negro fireman were both too drunk to be trusted with the engine. Anderson had the second section in order of movement, and he made arrangements with the crew of the third section to keep a sharp look-out for the rear end of his train. He then mounted the cab of the MONROE and kept his crew under some semblance of control until they sobered up enough to complete the run to Beaver Dam, Virginia, where the troops were detrained. After a wild and exciting trip, the train arrived safely and the weary skipper and his runner stretched out for some much-needed rest on the cold, wet floor of an empty freight car.

(Library of Congress photo, courtesy of Southern Railway)

27

VIRGINIA RAILROADING

This quiet scene shows two trains of the United States Military Railroad halted on the tracks of the Orange & Alexandria Railroad near Union Mills, Virginia. The stacked muskets in the left foreground and other evidence of camp life indicate that the Army has a guard detail stationed in the vicinity.

Some of the Orange & Alexandria road's men and equipment was involved in one of the worst train wrecks ever to take place on the lines operated under the Confederate flag.

In the spring of 1862 an Orange & Alexandria train arrived at Gordonsville and received orders to run over the Virginia Central tracks to Richmond. The message was urgent, reading: "Come to Richmond—moments are hours." The train was loaded with Confederate soldiers, needed urgently in the Peninsula, and also carried a number of refugees; it was headed by the engine JEFF DAVIS, captured on the Loudon & Hampshire road, and Engineer Amos Woodward was at the throttle. The colonel of a Louisiana outfit, under the influence of strong drink, was riding the cab and ordered the runner to open his throttle and to stop for nothing. About 11:00 P.M. the Virginia Central dispatcher started a westbound freight out of Richmond for Gordonsville in charge of Conductor John Richardson; this train was pulled by the heavy 4-6-0 freight engine MILLBORO, with Engineer Seth Mack at her throttle. Mack had orders to report to the operator at Hanover Junction (now Doswell), Virginia, where the eastbound troop special was also required by rule to stop and report. Ordered on by the tipsy Louisiana officer, the JEFF DAVIS and her crew rushed by Beaver Dam and on through the night. At Hanover Junction the operator tried in vain to flag them down. About five minutes later, in a curving cut near Little River, the special locked horns with the MILLBORO in a frightful crash; the old wooden cars of the 10-car special telescoped badly, killing many Confederate soldiers and refugees, including a number of women and children. Engineer Seth Mack survived the collision, but a great many of the boys in gray were not so fortunate and met their death not at the muzzles of Yankee guns, but through the stupidity of one of their own officers. Shortly after this tragedy, the Confederate Government issued orders that military officers should not interfere with railroad management.

YUBA DAM

When the U.S. Military Railroad operated the northern portion of the Richmond, Fredericksburg & Potomac Railroad, the landing at Aquia Creek was a focal point for rail and water shipping. To accommodate heavy loads of traffic, a branch line connected to the RF&P was built about a mile and a half below the Aquia Creek landing, and two wharves constructed there; the railroad wharf was 840 feet long and was connected to a wagon road wharf 380 feet long. These facilities were ordered built by General Burnside and the landing was called Burnside Wharf, but the operating railroaders named the site Yuba Dam. The work of constructing these wharves was under the supervision of Wm. W. Wright.

This view shows the Yuba Dam landing with freight cars on the railroad wharf and vessels, tugs, and barges lying alongside; in the right foreground, workmen are completing the wagon road wharf. The bank directly in-shore from the wharves was high and composed of a marly, shell-filled substance; to avoid the danger of slides from this bank, the branch railroad leading to the wharves was constructed on crib work erected in the river along the face of the bluff. The Yuba Dam and Aquia Creek landings played an important role in supplying the Army of the Potomac.

(Courtesy of the National Archives)

29

ALEXANDRIA SHOPS

This view of the machine shops operated by the United States Military Railroads in Alexandria, Virginia, was taken in March, 1863, and depicts an interesting phase of USMRR operations. In addition to ordinary repairs to locomotives and rolling stock, records indicate that the Government employees built a locomotive here for use on the Military Railroads. While it is possible that this engine, the NORTHERN LIGHT, was only a thorough rebuilding of some acquired locomotive, the records do not verify this; the locomotive in question was later renamed the GENL. SHERIDAN and was sold in 1865 to one William Phelps for a reported $13,500.

Another U.S. Military R.R. locomotive sold in 1865 was the D. H. RUCKER, built by New Jersey Loco. & Machine Co. in 1863 and probably named in honor of Col. Rucker of the Quartermaster Department. The D. H. RUCKER, with 16x24 inch cylinders and 60 inch driving wheels, went to the Baltimore & Ohio Railroad for $14,150.

Note the pairs of driving wheels on the track leading into the shops; the shop forces had plenty of work to keep them busy, as a sampling of USMRR accident reports will reveal. On one occasion Trains 5 and 8 met in a head-on collision, smashing both engines and 10 cars; not long after, Train No. 5 left a part of its cars on the main line where it was struck by

Train No. 10, breaking up the locomotive and 10 more cars.

Similar operating accidents took place in the Department of Mississippi. Between July 1st and July 25th, 1864, 12 accidents to trains were reported; of these 5 were collisions, 4 were derailments, and one a wreck caused by guerrillas removing a rail. One locomotive burst a flue and another train was captured by the Confederates and burned.

In spite of strict regulations forbidding the use of liquor by train and engine crews, some of the accidents were caused by intoxicated operating personnel, especially in the West. The use of liquor on the lines in Virginia was listed as a cause for prompt dismissal from the service, although the use of intoxicants in the Army was widespread and inebriation was no respecter of rank; if there seemed to be a higher ratio of intoxicated officers, it must be remembered that the low pay of the enlisted men was a contributing factor in limiting their use of hard liquor.

Engineers in the Western Departments who, through carelessness, caused derailments by running their locomotives through open stub switches were made to forfeit one week's wages, a ruling that probably contributed to more caution in engine operation.

READY FOR THE ADVANCE

When General Hooker replaced General Burnside as commander of the Army of the Potomac, he planned to move against the Confederates on the Rappahannock in a drive toward Richmond. Before the battle of Chancellorsville, Hooker sent for General Haupt and requested him to be prepared for rapid restoration of the Richmond, Fredericksburg & Potomac Railroad, which would be Hooker's main supply line. Haupt's construction crews had prepared about 1,600 lineal feet of bridges, 1,000 feet of which was composed of the prefabricated 60-foot long board spans of the type shown here. These "shad-belly" trusses were to be hauled by rail to the end of track, then moved by oxen to the bridge sites and raised into position with an apparatus specially devised for the purpose. About 70 car loads of railroad repair material was readied for Hooker's "On To Richmond" movement when the battle of Chancellorsville changed Hooker's plans; General Haupt remarked that: ". . . the enemy was so unaccommodating as not to give us an opportunity of using them."

In the interval before Chancellorsville, Haupt replaced the old Potomac Run trestle with a new truss bridge; three spans of the new military type truss were erected in about a day and a half, without a minute's delay to the heavy flow of trains.

(Courtesy of the National Archives)

(Courtesy of the National Archives)

DESTRUCTION

This view shows one of the methods devised by Herman Haupt in his experiments to determine the most practical manner by which to destroy enemy rail lines. By placing one end of a rail against an anchored rail and using a pin set into a hole bored in a tie for a fulcrum, a rail could be readily bent by hitching a horse to the long end of the rail and pulling it around. Rails bent and broken by this method appear in this photograph.

REPARATION

Rails which had been only slightly bent out of shape by enemy action could be repaired by this method devised by Haupt's Construction Corps. A gang of contraband laborers simply raised the damaged iron rail to shoulder height and, at a command, let it drop across a timber placed on the ground. By repeating this process a few times, minor bends could be straightened enough to permit the rail to be used again in reconstruction of damaged track.

31

MILITARY STEAMER
Engine No. 137 of the United States Military Railroad was one of the 5-foot gauge locomotives built for use on the lines in the West in 1864. This photo of the Danforth, Cooke & Company 4-4-0 woodburner was taken near the enginehouse of the U.S. Military Railroad in Chattanooga, Tennessee.

(Courtesy of the National Archives)

MILITARY RAILROAD BRASS

This group of U.S. Military Railroad Superintendents and Foremen posed long enough to have their images recorded on the glass plate of a Civil War photographer, but their names and the date are not recorded; the view was probably taken in Virginia, but the place is unknown.

The majority of the men who directed the Military Railroad operations were of high caliber and devoted to their duties; one exception noted in the operations in the West was the case of a foreman who indulged in petty graft by padding his ration returns and by selling discharges to the men contracted to work on the construction details.

As of January 1st, 1865, the following officers commanded the United States Military Railroads: D. C. McCallum, Director & General Manager; Adna Anderson, Chief Supt. & Engr. (after the War Anderson served as Chief Engr. of Construction during the building of the Northern Pacific Railroad); J. J. Moore, Chief Engr., Alexandria, Va.; J. McCallum, Supt., Alexandria; O. A. Torrance, Supt., Harpers Ferry; H. F. Woodward, Supt., Norfolk, Va.; G. M. Huntingdon, Supt., City Point, Va.; E. L. Wentz, General Supt., Nashville, Tenn.; W. W. Wright, Chief Engr., Chattanooga, Tenn.; Supt. Tallmadge, Chattanooga; W. J. Stevens, Supt., Nashville; A. F. Goodhue, Supt., Memphis; and E. D. Butler, Supt., Vicksburg, Mississippi.

The Memphis superintendency covered the Mobile & Ohio from Columbus to Union City and the Memphis & Charleston Railroad from Memphis to Girard Junction. Supt. Butler had charge of the Vicksburg and Jackson line and Supt. Torrance controlled the 28 miles of the Winchester & Potomac Railroad between Harpers Ferry and Stevenson.

(Courtesy of the Pennsylvnia Railroad)

EFFICIENT BRASS HAT

Thomas A. Scott, a native Pennsylvanian, began his railroading on the Pennsylvania R.R. in 1850 at the age of 27. He was serving as agent at Hollidaysburg when Gen. Supt. Herman Haupt recommended he be promoted to Assistant Superintendent. Scott rose rapidly in the ranks of officialdom and by March of 1860 he was a Vice President of the Pennsy. Called to the office of Governor Curtin at the outbreak of the Civil War, he opened the first military telegraph office with a key placed on the sill of an office window. Scott's able aide was a young Scotchman, Andrew Carnegie, who had entered the service of the Pennsylvania in the Pittsburg telegraph office at the age of 16. Carnegie, destined to become a noted figure on the American scene, had been appointed Scott's private secretary and telegrapher; it was Carnegie who, at Scott's direction, recruited four telegraph operators from the ranks of Pennsy brass-pounders to form the nucleus of the Military Telegraph Corps. The four chosen were from Pittsburg, Breensburg, Altoona, and Mifflin, Penna.

In May of 1861 Thos. Scott was commissioned a Colonel of Volunteers and placed in charge of railroads and telegraph lines used by the Federal armies. He was a friend of Secretary of War Cameron and in August of 1861 was appointed Asst. Sec. of War, his former railroad duties passing to Capt. R. N. Morley of the Quartermaster Dept. Scott was responsible for building the railroad through the streets of Washington to form a northern link between the Orange & Alexandria and the northern roads via the Long Bridge across the Potomac.

When Edwin M. Stanton replaced Cameron as Secretary of War, Scott lost some of his influence; he had wrangled with President Garrett of the Baltimore & Ohio, but the men later patched up their difficulties and worked together to keep the trains of war rolling.

Scott advised the creation of transportation and telegraph bureaus to take charge of military communications and railroad and water transport; he helped plan the large-scale movements of troops to the western theater of the War, and prepared reports of transportation problems. As Assistant Secretary of War, he tried to arrange draft exemptions for all civilian railroaders, knowing how vital the experienced men were in the operation of the railroads burdened with the rush of war traffic; action by the Government exempted locomotive engineers from the draft, and some sorely-needed mechanics were released to civilian duty, but the nation's rail lines were hampered by the loss of experienced men called to the colors by the draft demands.

Scott's long service as President of the Pennsylvania Railroad after his war duties ended need not be recounted here; he built a fine record as one of the outstanding rail officials of his day.

G.I. MOTIVE POWER

The United States Military Railroad locomotive shown here is the GEO. A. PARKER, a Baldwin built for the Government in 1862; she may have been named in honor of George A. Parker, former Chief Engineer of the Philadelphia, Wilmington & Baltimore Railroad. In this photo, probably taken at Alexandria, Virginia, the PARKER is sporting a metal pilot.

The locomotives of the Military Railroads in Virginia bore names and those used in the West carried numbers, but some of the numbered engines were acquired second-hand and retained the names applied by previous ownrs. U.S.M.R.R. Engines No. 6, WILLIAMSON, No. 22, NASHVILLE, and No. 224, FRANKLIN, were acquired from the Tennessee & Alabama Railroad; No. 69, MAURY, and No. 99, THOS. BUFORD, came from the Central Southern Railroad, while No. 229, LUKE PRIOR, was from the Tennessee & Alabama Central Railroad. These three roads formed the Nashville & Decatur line from the Tennessee capital to Decatur, Alabama. The Tennessee & Alabama ran from Nashville to Mt. Pleasant, Tennessee; the Central Southern Railroad left the Tennessee & Alabama at Columbia and ran to the Alabama-Tennessee state boundary, where it connected with the Tennessee & Alabama Central Railroad, the latter road forming the link to Decatur, Alabama, where it joined the Memphis & Charleston. The Tennessee & Alabama line from Columbia to Mt. Pleasant, 12 miles, was torn up by the Federal forces, who also removed about 27 miles of rail from the 35-mile long McMinnville & Manchester Railroad which ran from Tullahoma to McMinnville, Tennessee.

Other engines purchased for use in Tennessee included the WASH GRAHAM, a Taunton acquired from an unknown source, and the SLATER, another Taunton purchased from the Cleveland & Pittsburg Railroad.

Contemporary reports of Civil War days state that the Government acquired a 4-6-0 from the Cleveland, Columbus & Cincinnati Railroad in 1863 and that the Sandusky, Dayton & Cincinnati sold one of their locomotives to the Government in the same year.

A locomotive purchased from the St. Louis, Alton & Terre Haute Railroad for service on the Military Railroads was reportedly lost overboard while being transported down the Ohio River.

The Government purchased two Mason engines, the LITTLE ROCK and the MEMPHIS, for use on the Memphis & Little Rock Railroad operations in Arkansas in 1865, along with the GENERAL STEELE, a Taunton product; they also acquired the GENERAL REYNOLDS for use on this line, a Manchester which may have been purchased second-hand. These four locomotives were later sold but no record apparently exists regarding their purchasers.

(Courtesy of Ansco Brady collection)

35

(Library of Congress, courtesy of Association of American Railroads)

YANKEE WHEELS IN VIRGINIA

The locomotive FIREFLY of the United States Military Railroad poses for the photographer on the Orange & Alexandria Railroad near Union Mills, Virginia. The 4-4-0 was built for Federal use by R. Norris & Son of Philadelphia in 1862, and after the War was over she was sold to the Baltimore & Ohio Railroad for $12,500.

The wooden frame trestle in this picture was erected to replace the destroyed bridge that originally spanned the creek between the two stone abutments. Much of the reconstruction work in Virginia for the Military Railroad was supervised by E. C. Smeed, who was one of General Herman Haupt's most trusted officials. Before the start of the War, Smeed had been Road Supervisor for the Catawissa Railroad in Pennsylvania, where he had charge of bridges and trestles. He came to Virginia in the early days of the War to serve as foreman of bridge carpenters under Daniel Stone, and was assigned to Haupt's command on the Richmond, Fredericksburg & Potomac, where Haupt was quick to recognize his qualities; he was placed in general charge of erecting the noted Potomac Run trestle, one of the construction wonders of its day. Although Smeed lacked formal education he studied hard and became an expert mathematician; his ingenuity was responsible for the iron hooks he invented for the quick destruction of rails and track. Smeed was by nature rather reserved, slow, diffident, and did not make friends quickly, but Haupt recounted that the man was the best organizer he ever saw, and that his spirit encouraged his gangs to carry out prodigious feats. His work in the Department of Tennessee is recounted elsewhere in these pages. After the War ended, Smeed became Chief Engineer for the Kansas Pacific Railroad; Haupt, serving as General Manager of construction on the new transcontinental Northern Pacific Railroad in 1881, tried to secure Smeed's services, but the canny Jay Gould recognized Smeed's value and out-bid Haupt's proferred wage offer by $4,000.

POPE'S RUN

Soldiers and civilians appear in this photo taken at the trestle over the Virginia stream known as Pope's Run. As the tides of war swept back and forth over the Virginia countryside many railroad bridges and trestles were destroyed and then rebuilt, only to be destroyed again. Much of the timber used in the reconstruction was cut from the surrounding woods, causing large areas to become denuded before the War ended.

(Courtesy of the National Archives)

37

BULL RUN BRIDGE

(Courtesy of National Archives)

This photo shows one of the seven bridges erected across Bull Run on the Orange & Alexandria Railroad during the Civil War. Six were destroyed in the course of military action and the seventh, a temporary timber trestle, was washed out in a freshet that swept the supporting timbers from the bottom of the stream but left the rails above intact.

General Haupt's Construction Corps adapted the style of military truss bridge shown here for a number of important reasons. The structure could be used either as a deck bridge, with rails laid on the top of the bridge, or as through truss span, with the tracks running through the bridge as in this installation. Perhaps the most important feature of the bridge was that it could be easily assembled to any length desired, and the job could be done by unskilled labor. The timbers were all alike and interchangeable, and could be reversed end for end and still fit together. The material could be cut far in

advance of the time needed and stored until ready for use; the bridge needed no pre-construction, all parts being made so as to permit them to be assembled at the bridge site. Only saws and augers were needed by the crewmen, in addition to a set of block and tackle for hoisting the timbers into position.

The ease and rapidity with which this type of bridge could be assembled was also an important feature; General Haupt estimated that one of these pre-cut spans could be erected in one-half or even one-third the amount of time required to raise any other type of bridge.

The plans for this type of bridge were drawn while the Corps was quartered at Alexandria, Virginia, and the work of erecting the structures could be prosecuted so rapidly that Haupt's bridge foreman, E. C. Smeed, expressed his humorous opinion that he could assemble such a bridge about as fast as a dog could trot.

WAR IS HELL

A 32-pound shell from a gun of the Second Massachusetts Heavy Artillery created the havoc shown here at the battle of Fredericksburg. This photograph, taken May 3rd, 1863, shows General Herman Haupt (at left) and Supt. W. W. Wright of the U.S. Military Railroad surveying the dead artillery horses on the field of battle. Haupt and Wright, accompanied by Army photographic artist Capt. A. J. Russell, examined the bloody ground while the battle was still in progress and the two Army railroaders narrowly escaped death or capture on May 4th. Unknown to Haupt, rebel troops had occupied a line of ditch, screened by trees and a fence, not far from the depot of the Richmond, Fredericksburg & Potomac Railroad. At some distance from the station there was a pile of lumber and Haupt and Wright, both dressed in civilian clothing, strolled out to examine this lumber to see if it could be used as bridge material. Riflemen in the ditch beyond were keeping up a steady fire, and Haupt supposed they were Union troops. Returning to the depot, the two railroaders were leisurely strolling along the tracks and wondering why the dead bodies had not been buried when they came upon some Yankee soldiers sheltered behind a building. Haupt approached them and asked what the men in the ditch were firing at. "Popping at us when we shows ourselves," was the reply. "Them's the rebs."

Wright and Haupt had unwittingly walked nearly into the Confederate lines, and Haupt assumed later that their civilian clothing and apparent boldness had led the rebels to believe that he and Wright were loyal Southern residents of Fredericksburg, thus allowing them to stroll across the battlefield unharmed.

MEN AT WORK

Members of the Construction Corps are shown here repairing the wooden trestle across Bull Run on the Orange & Alexandria Railroad, probably after it had been damaged by a freshet. The car wheels in the stream in two locations and the car trucks in the lower left foreground testify to the fact that some of the rolling stock of the Military Railroad operations has come to grief at this site. The vulnerability of wooden railroad spans made them frequent targets for the armies of both North and South.

(Courtesy of the National Archives)

(Courtesy of Ansco Brady collection)

39

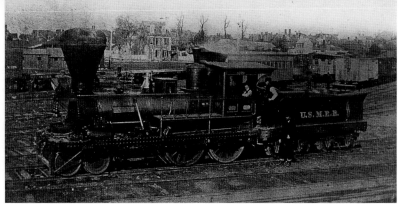

BATTLE VETERAN

The U.S. Military Railroad engine DOVER was a 4-4-0 with outside frames and was acquired second-hand from the Boston & Maine Railroad. She was built by Hinkley & Drury in 1856, along with the EXETER; note the goose-neck coupling link hanging on the side of her tender. On August 27th, 1862, while runinng on the war-torn Orange & Alexandria Railroad, the DOVER was fired into by Confederates along the track a mile or two west of Burke's Station. Only a few days before, the crew of Train No. 6, headed by the engine SECRETARY, had been involved in a brush with a force of Confederate cavalry, numbering about 500, at Catlett's Station on the same road. As the train approached the station, the engineer noted a pile of ties on the track and instantly realized he was into a rebel ambush. He peeled his throttle wide open and the locomotive scattered the obstruction and wheeled on through to safety. The Confederates peppered the fleeing train with a hail of bullets but the crew escaped injury by throwing themselves flat; General Haupt noted in his report that the SECRETARY was well riddled by the enemy fire. A short time later the SECRETARY struck the rear end of a preceding train about 2 miles from the Bull Run bridge, the accident blocking the road.

The action along the Orange & Alexandria in August of 1862 kept the Military railroaders extremely busy. During the retreat of General John Pope's forces, Haupt's men lost a large quantity of rolling stock to the rebels at Bristoe, and Haupt himself narrowly escaped capture, the train behind the one in which he was riding being taken by the Confederates. Unsung heroes of the campaign were Conductor C. M. Strein and James J. Moore, Asst. Engineer of the Construction Corps,

along with their crews. Conductor Strein's train, drawn by the Baldwin-built engine, VULCAN, moved Moore's construction force into the hostile region between the two armies. From the crude materials at hand, the workmen rebuilt the Pohick Creek bridge which had been burned by the Confederates. Moving cautiously forward into area swarming with rebel troops, Strein and his party succeeded in bringing back a full train load of Union wounded, survivors of the action at Fairfax. This evacuation was carried out in the face of an enemy force about 20,000 strong, and is typical of the bravery and courageous initiative of Army railroad men.

EXPERIMENTAL SPAN

When winter slowed the activities of the armies in the field, General Herman Haupt kept his Construction Corps occupied around the Alexandria terminal.

Several types of board trusses were constructed, but in general they all followed the same basic principle; boards 12 inches wide and 1 inch thick were spiked and bolted together to form trusses 6 feet high and 60 feet long. Planks 2 inches thick were used to form the bracing between the upper and lower fish-shaped arches. Haupt's men built a suspension span, shown in this photograph, by placing two of these board trusses side by side and decking the upper arch to carry a railroad track. Rails were piled on the span and in a further test, a flat car loaded with 20 tons of rail was pulled onto the span. After supporting a weight of 108,000 pounds for 5 min-

utes, the span broke; in the next experiment the boards forming the chords had their surfaces pitched, to provide greater adhesion. Extra thicknesses of boards were included in the truss members, and this new span broke only when loaded with a weight of about 105 tons.

Haupt's report stated that two of these board trusses would successfully support a locomotive, and that the bridges could be assembled on the bank of a stream, drawn across by a capstan while floating on the water, then raised and supported on barges or pontoons to form a suitable bridge.

(Courtesy of National Archives)

HOME FRONT DEFENSE

Herman Haupt detailed his Construction Corps to erect these palisades around the yards and machine shops of the Orange & Alexandria Railroad at the Alexandria, Virginia, terminal. The barricades were designed to shelter the Military Railroad personnel and equipment in case of a raid by the swift-moving forces of the Confederate Army.

The staff of the Military Railroad had to guard against the enemy within as well as the regular Confederate forces. At Alexandria, a civilian employee in the Orange & Alexandria shops named William Hook was ordered arrested, suspected of being a rebel sympathizer and charged with hiding vital parts of the locomotives in the shops for servicing and repairs, thus rendering the engines unfit for use. Hook's case was not the only attempt at sabotage encountered by the Army railroaders. Haupt cited the affair of the Fredericksburg shops to P. H. Watson, Assistant Secretary of War, and received instructions from Watson to arrest anyone involved in similar circumstances. When the Military Railroad occupied Fredericksburg, the shop forces took charge of a machine shop there and began to use their facilities. After having used the forges for two days, Master Mechanic M. P. Wood and his blacksmith gang discovered that a loaded shell had been placed in each forge. Haupt believed that the civilian proprietor of the shops, John Scott, was guilty of this attempted sabotage and advised Watson that the man should be arrested and not released.

QUICK REPAIRS

General Haupt devised the method shown here for removing short bends or kinks from rails, whether in place in the track or out of it. Two solid pieces of timber were held in position by metal rods and pressure on the bent rail was applied by the jackscrew, forcing the rail into a very fair degree of straightness.

The pile of iron rails in the background had been damaged by the Confederates on the Loudon & Hampshire Railroad and were removed to Alexandria for salvage; a number of them had been heated and wrapped around trees, which had to be cut down in order to permit the removal of the rails.

(Courtesy of the National Archives)

MILITARY RAILROAD VIEWS

These three scenes were on the lines of the Orange & Alexandria Railroad in Virginia during the control of that line by the U.S. Military Railroads. The upper right photo shows the Alexandria machine shops and the east yard of the O. & A. R.R.; three sets of three-way stub switches can be seen in this picture. The upper left photo, taken from the roof of the roundhouse, shows the offices of the Orange & Alexandria R.R., with Fort Lyon in the distance. The lower photo shows the crude pole and sod huts in the forest along the O. & A. R.R. which sheltered the wood choppers engaged in cutting wood for the Military Railroad locomotives. This fuel was supplied under the supervision of Major Brayton. Wood for engine fuel was a problem and the Louisville & Nashville tried coal as a fuel in 1862-63, but the difficulty in obtaining it forced the road to return to wood. Assisted by the military, the L. & N. conscripted about 500 slaves in each of the 13 counties where the road operated and used them to cut wood for the locomotive fuel supply.

(Three photos, Virginia Historical Society, courtesy of National Archives)

VIRGINIA RAIL STATIONS

At upper right is a view of a U.S. Military Railroad locomotive switching at Fairfax Station on the Orange & Alexandria R.R., while this point was the main supply depot for the Army of the Potomac in March, 1863. At upper left is a view of the Warrenton, Virginia, depot and yards, showing an engine and freight cars. This station on the Orange & Alexandria R.R. was located at the end of a branch running westerly from the main line from Warrenton Junction, between Catlett's Station and Bealeton. Photo at lower right shows a freight train on the Orange & Alexandria R.R. near Culpeper Court House in August, 1862, taken by Timothy H. O'Sullivan.

(Upper right photo, courtesy of Ansco Brady Collection; upper left and lower photos, courtesy of Library of Congress)

44

ONE FOR THE "OLD MAN"

This photo taken at the Alexandria roundhouse in 1863 shows the Mason-built locomotive GENL. HAUPT, named in honor of the guiding genius of the Military Railroad operations. In 1862 the Military Superintendent in charge of the confiscated Orange & Alexandria Railroad at Alexandria was John H. Devereux, one of the best men in the service. Haupt was out on the Manassas Gap Railroad and became greatly aroused when the trains failed to move promptly from the Alexandria terminal. At the time he was not fully acquainted with Devereux and sent a wire demanding an explanation of the delay, threatening to remove Devereux from his position. In reply, Devereux reported that all except five of the locomotives were out on the Manassas Gap road where military interference was causing blockades. Of the five engines remaining under Devereux's supervision, the Super stated that the confiscated 4-6-0 of the Orange & Alexandria, the RAPIDAN, was the only one fit for the heavy transfer work between Washington and Alexandria. The old FAIRFAX, a Smith & Perkins product built in 1851, was in such poor shape that she could be used only as an emergency switch engine; a few days before she had been pressed into main line service, broke down, and tied the road up for hours. The INDIANA, a Baldwin built in 1846, was also in very poor condition, fit only for yard work but occasionally pressed into road service. This left only the DELAWARE and the CAPT. FERGUSON to bear the brunt of the heavy traffic. In addition, Devereux noted that there was but one telegraph operator at the terminal and that this man was on duty 24 hours a day. Haupt was quick to realize Devereux's problems and the two were to become close friends in the days that followed.

––––––––––––•––––––––––––

BRIDGE DEMOLITION

This photograph taken by Capt. A. J. Russell illustrates Herman Haupt's experiments in railroad bridge destruction conducted near Alexandria, Virginia. Two men with augers are boring holes in the wooden truss, while the man seated at right holds the torpedo device to be inserted into the holes. Haupt recommended a fuze about 2 feet long for detonating the charge of powder in the torpedo, and added that an ordinary cigar lighter which burned without flame and could not be blown out was best suited for igniting the fuze.

In his report of November, 1862, covering the use of torpedoes for bridge demolition, Haupt also mentioned that it had been the practice to destroy locomotives by draining the boilers and then building a fire in the firebox, burning the dry crownsheets. He commented that this method was poor, as the enemy soon repaired the engines thus damaged, and stated that a better method woud be to fire a cannon ball through the boiler. The destruction of freight cars was best accomplished by fire and Haupt reported that Federal troops had burned more than 400 cars in the previous six months.

(Courtesy of the National Archives)

ONE FOR THE SUPER

(Courtesy of Library of Congress)

This superb old photograph shows the locomotive, J. H. DEVEREUX of the United States Military Railroad, named in honor of John H. Devereux, who held the position of Superintendent at Alexandria, Virginia. Devereux was a warm personal friend of General McCallum and when Herman Haupt took charge of the military line operations, there was a decided coolness between the two but they later became good friends. Haupt admired Devereux's qualities as a railroad man, stating that he was a master of transportation details and of great physical endurance, being able to remain on duty for nights in succession without sleep. Devereux was also an active churchman, of the Episcopal faith, and his Christian beliefs helped cement the friendship with Haupt, a religious man who was married to a preacher's daughter. After the War ended,

Devereux became General Superintendent of the Cleveland & Pittsburgh Railroad and later became a railroad president, holding the job until his death.

The J. H. DEVEREUX was built by the New Jersey Locomotive & Machine Co. at their shops in Paterson, N.J., in 1863, and she was one of the most ornate engines on the Military Railroad's roster. Note the elaborate scroll-work on headlight and bell stand, the fancy nameplate between the drivers, and the artistic designs painted on her truck wheels, mud guards, and cab panels. On her sand dome is a fine colored oil portrait of John H. Devereux, a very remarkable likeness of the bearded official in whose honor the engine was named. The fireboy of the DEVEREUX is seated in the arched cab window and her bearded runner, oiler in hand, is in the gangway.

46

CAPITAL STATION

This view shows the depot of the Washington & Alexandria Railroad located on Maryland Avenue in Washington, D.C., at it appeared during the Civil War. This 7-mile pike carried a very heavy burden of military traffic between the National Capital and the connection with the Orange & Alexandria Railroad at Alexandria. From January 1st to June 30th, 1864, a total of 1,424 cars of troops and equipment moved over the line; in the period from June 30th of 1864 to June 30th of 1865, the road transported 132,335 men in military movements.

(Courtesy of Ansco Brady collection)

(Courtesy of Harold F. Fagerberg)

B&O TROOPER

This view at Keyser, West Virginia, reportedly shows a troop train bound toward Harper's Ferry in 1862. The locomotive is Baltimore & Ohio's No. 230, one of the famous Tyson 4-6-0 types. Feeling ran high in the border states during the War, with many residents pledging their loyalty to the Union and others embracing the State's Rights-Secession policy of the Confederate States of America.

47

PIONEER CAR FERRY

The United States Military Railroad operated the car floats shown here on the Potomac River; in the background is the steamer used to tow them to their destination. General Herman Haupt wrote the following description of this operation:

"(This photograph) Illustrates a mode of transportation which was adopted with great advantage on the Potomac in establishing a communication between Alexandria and Aquia Creek. It can be used to connect the various roads which have their termini on navigable rivers, and would prove of great advantage on the Western waters. The floats used on the Potomac consisted of two large sized Schuylkill barges, across which long timbers were placed supporting eight tracks. On these tracks loaded cars were run at Alexandria, towed to Aquia Creek, landed without break of bulk, and sent to advanced stations, where their contents were distributed. At the time of the abandonment of the Fredericksburg Railroad, in June, 1863, supplies from Falmouth and other stations in the front were loaded in cars, the cars run on floats at Aquia Creek, sent at Alexandria, landed without break of bulk, and sent forward to meet the Army which had marched overland to the line of the Orange & Alexandria Railroad. All the cars and engines were safely removed, and none of the stores lost or destroyed. Without the floats this would have been impossible."

Haupt's report went on to state that this method saved waste and expenses, reduced the risk of capture of supplies in the face of enemy advances, and suggested that opportunities for similar operations might exist on the Ohio and Mississippi Rivers.

ALEXANDRIA WHARF

This view shows the wharf facilities used by the United States Military Railroad at Alexandria, Virginia, on the Potomac River. At right are two of the bulky Schuylkill barges with tracks laid across them for ferrying cars and locomotives to the landings at Aquia Creek. At the outer end of the wharf are the three slips used for loading the rolling stock onto the barges for shipment. A woodburner of the Military Railroad is standing on the wharf, but the ramp hides the identity of the old 4-4-0 with outside frames; she is probably one of the older locomotives purchased second-hand by the Government from some of the Northern railroads.

The float lying alongside the wharf in the right foreground contains a small hoisting and pumping engine. In his report on Military Railroad operations, Haupt noted that several of these engines were used to supply water stations. This photograph is one of a number taken by Captain A. J. Russell to illustrate the Haupt report.

TRANSFER POINT

This photograph by Captain A. J. Russell shows the outer end of the wharf at Alexandria, on the Potomac River. It was taken from the deck of the Schuylkill barges as they were about to be warped into position for loading freight cars for shipment by water; the sections of track laid on the decks of the barges can be plainly seen in the right foreground. The three slips or aprons could be raised or lowered to the proper height to permit the cars to be shoved onto the waiting barges; at the time this picture was taken, only the center slip had rails laid on it. General Haupt stated that these slips, or "bridges," were rough and imperfect, but that they answered the purpose for which they were intended and greatly increased the facilities for loading and unloading the rolling stock.

In the background stands one of the older locomotives used by the United States Military Railroad, a 4-4-0 with outside frames typical of motive power in use in the 1850's.
(Courtesy of National Archives)

BLACK GOLD

This woodburner of the Oil Creek Railroad was photographed near Rouseville, Pennsylvania, by John A. Mather while switching the oil wells during the Civil War. Note the barrels of crude oil loaded on flat cars, forerunners of the modern tank cars.

Col. Edwin Drake, a New York & New Haven Railroad conductor, drilled the first successful commercial oil well near Titusville, Pennsylvania, in 1859 and the Civil War boomed the industry. Petroleum was used to lubricate the Yankee war machinery, and oil derivatives were used for illumination, fuel, and even for medicinal purposes. Exports of oil to Europe leaped from 37,000 barrels in 1861 to 770,000 barrels in 1863, bringing a flow of gold to bolster the sagging economy of the North. In 1864-65, the Federal taxes received from oil exceeded those from both iron and coal.

From dozens of flimsy derricks such as those pictured here, railroaders hauled trains loaded with the explosive crude oil from the Northern oil fields, strengthening the finances of the Union and aiding in the struggle to suppress the Rebellion.
(Courtesy of A. C. Thompson, Curator, Drake Well Park Museum)

49

GRACEFUL MASON

Posed at the roundhouse in Alexandria, Virginia, is the locomotive CLARKE of the U.S. Military Railroads. This engine is believed to have been the CHARLES P. MANNING of the Alexandria, Loudon & Hampshire Railroad, built by Wm. Mason, Shop No. 85, in 1859. Another Mason engine on the AL&H when the road was taken over by the Military Railroads was the LEWIS McKENZIE, Mason Shop No. 80, built in October, 1858. Typical of the Mason design, the CLARKE has no visible counterbalances in her driving wheels, the necesssary weights being concealed to help preserve Mason's ideals of symmetry in the styling of his engines.

The 4-4-0 or American type of wheel arrangement was the most commonly used design on the Military Railroads, but was not used exclusively. Engine 27, built by Baldwin in October of 1863 for service in the West was an 0-6-0 type with link motion; No. 29, a Baldwin built in November of 1863 was an 0-4-0 type. Another Baldwin, built in 1864, was Engine No. 90, a 4-6-0 type.

In 1865 several locomotives were captured on local rail lines in North Carolina which came under U.S. Military Railroad control. The PERSEVERANCE, a Baldwin 0-8-0 of 1849, and the NORTH CAROLINA, a Baldwin 0-6-0 of 1850, were bagged on the Wilmington & Weldon R.R.; the Raleigh & Gaston yielded a pair of small 2-4-0 types, the RALEIGH, an R. Norris engine built between 1848 and 1850, and the TORNADO, built by D. J. Burr & Co. in 1838.

D. J. Burr & Co. was established in Richmond, Virginia, about 1838. Other locomotive builders in the South included Burr, Pea & Sampson; Burr & Ettinger; Talbott & Brothers; Anderson & Delany; and the later Tredegar Works in Richmond. The Appomattox Locomotive Works was located in Petersburg, Virginia, and the Virginia Locomotive & Car Manufacturing Co. and Smith & Perkins were located in Alexandria. Early builders of locomotives in Charleston, South Carolina, included Eason & Dotterer, E. L. Miller, and McLeish & Smith.

CIVIL WAR SWITCHER

The 0-4-0 tank engine pictured here is a Baldwin owned by the Cumberland Valley R.R. and named the FRANKLIN. The Cumberland Valley R.R. and the Franklin R.R. joined at Chambersburg, forming a line between Harrisburg, Pennsylvania, and Hagerstown, Maryland. These lines, along with the Northern Central R.R., the Hanover Branch R.R., the Hanover & Gettysburg R.R.,. and the 9½-mile branch from Hanover to Littlestown, Pa., all were involved in the Gettysburg campaign.

(Courtesy of Thomas Norrell)

(Courtesy of the Library of Congress)

MAN OF ACTION

Herman Haupt constantly moved in the van of railroad operations under his control in the Civil War, no detail being too small to escape his eye. In this photo Haupt is the jack-booted figure with beard and black slouch hat supervising excavation for a wye at Devereux Station on the Orange & Alexandria Railroad; the locomotive heading up the work train was named GENL. HAUPT in his honor. Note the water boy passing a dipper of water from his pail to the thirsty laborer standing beside the flat cars used to haul off the spoil.

Haupt had no fear of Army "brass," and when conditions demanded, he routed generals from their beds without a qualm. He once turned General Hancock out of bed about midnight to get a guard for a train he wanted moved into dangerous territory near Bull Run, and when a freight blockade at Piedmont was holding up his precious supply of freight cars, he persuaded General McDowell to send his Chief Quartermaster and Chief Commissary from Rectortown, 4 miles away, in a driving night rainstorm to supervise and speed up the unloading of supplies by their men. When Secretary of War Stanton tried to make the military railroaders sign receipts for supplies shipped by rail, Haupt objected so strongly that the order was not enforced; Haupt took the position that the stores were loaded and unloaded by Commissary and Quartermaster forces, and that they were the ones responsible for the material. He cited the fact that Army guards broke into hospital cars and drank the liquor intended for medicinal purposes, a situation over which his operating crews had no control. Quick to place blame where it belonged, Haupt was equally quick to praise. In his memoirs he had kind words for his subordinates, including Bridge Foreman Geo. Speer; G. W. Nagle and his three brothers; Tinglepaugh, who managed the Construction Corps' herd of work oxen that were known as "Haupt's horned cavalry"; and the loyal engine and train crews, including many conductors brought down from the Pennsylvania Railroad by Thomas Scott.

ENDLESS TASK

Members of the Construction Corps are shown here replacing a destroyed railroad bridge across Cedar Run, near Catlett's Station, Virginia. Much of the war-time action on the Orange & Alexandria Railroad centered around the portion of the road between Fairfax and Culpeper and the intermediate stations at Manassas Junction, Bealeton, Brandy Station, and on the Warrenton Junction-Warrenton branch. Among the streams bridged by the Construction Corps were Pole-cat Run, Licking Run, Winter Branch, and Marsh Run.

(Courtesy of the Library of Congress)

TWO RAILROAD CLASSICS

This lovely old photograph shows the U.S. Military Railroad locomotive W. H. WHITON and the private car built by the Military Railroad for President Abraham Lincoln. The engine was built by Wm. Mason in 1862, and was named in honor of William H. Whiton, Chief Clerk for the U.S. Military Railroads. General Haupt recalled that Whiton was well educated, very intelligent, and of independent financial circumstances. He married a daughter of President Lord of the Erie Railroad and owned a fine estate on the Hudson near Piermont. Whiton, a thorough accountant, entered the service because of his patriotism and a warm personal friendship for General Dan McCallum.

A great deal of controversy centers about the Lincoln car. In 1893, W. H. H. Price, former foreman of the U.S. Military Railroad car shops at Alexandria, Virginia, was holding the position of Master Car Builder for the East Tennessee, Virginia & Georgia Ry. at Knoxville, Tennessee. He wrote an article for the Railroad Car Journal, stating that the idea for the car was conceived by B. P. Lamison, Supt. of the U.S. Military Railroad car works in Virginia, in 1863. Price related that the car was completed at Alexandria in February, 1865. Sidney D. King, Asst. Master Car Builder for the Military Railroad, also stated that the car was built inside the famous Haupt stockade at Alexandria, and both he and Price maintained that it was not armor-plated, as some stories indicated.

Even the disposition of the car is in doubt, some sources claiming that it was acquired by the Union Pacific shortly after Lincoln's death and taken West to Omaha.

(Courtesy of National Archives)

RAILROAD JUNCTION

This Civil War view from the files of the National Archives reportedly shows the junction of the Alexandria, Loudon & Hampshire Railroad with the Alexandria & Washington Railroad. The doubleheader at the right has been clearing up a wreck caused by a broken axle on a freight car; the engine coupled to the string of flats at left is the GEO. A. PARKER of the United States Military Railroads, built by Baldwin in 1862.

When Colonel D. C. McCallum took charge of the Government's rail operations in 1862, the 7-mile line of the Alexandria & Washington was the sole road under his control. It had been operated by Captain R. F. Morley, an assistant quartermaster, and connected Washington, D.C., with Alexandria, Virginia; cars had been moved across the bridge over the Potomac by horse-power. In 1862 this road was reorganized as the Washington, Alexandria & Georgetown Railroad.

The Alexandria, Loudon & Hampshire Railroad had been opened from Alexandria to Leesburg, Virginia, in the summer of 1858. This road, commonly known as the Loudon & Hampshire, was an important supply line to the Army of the Potomac in the fall of 1862. Not all of the problems of war-time rail operations could be credited to the forces of the enemy. In his report to Herman Haupt, Superintendent J. J. Moore complained that the Union troops stationed along the Loudon & Hampshire had broken a number of that road's switch stands and were wasting the line's supply of water and wood. Far worse, as the locomotive engineers and firemen on the road could profanely testify, was the troops' habit of bathing and doing their laundry in the water supply for the engines.

The quantities of soap used in bathing and washing caused the locomotive boilers to foam extensively, messing up the polished jackets and frequently causing the trains to come to a halt until the frothy mass could be blown down and the proper level of water restored over the crownsheets.

Rails of the Loudon & Hampshire continued to serve throughout the war, carrying mail and supply trains and also wood trains bound for the Quartermaster Department in Washington. Early in 1865, the victorious Army of the Potomac was encamped along the line prior to the discharge of its members.

55

RAIL TWISTER

In an attempt to discover the most practical method of destroying rails, Herman Haupt and his Construction Corps conducted a series of experiments at Alexandria, Virginia, in the winter of 1862-63. When time permitted, ties had been stacked and the rails piled across them, then the wood had been fired and the heated rails could be wrapped around a convenient tree. Haupt did not think this method entirely satisfactory, especially when used on raids behind the enemy lines where the time element was involved; the fires were slow to burn in the wet seasons, and forces had to remain at hand to tend them and to destroy the rails after heating. Rails piled across the pyres and left simply drooped slightly and could be straightened for re-use without much difficulty.

Haupt was also seeking a device to rip the rails from their position on the ties, and one of his most able officers came up with an invention that solved both of these problems. E. C. Smeed rushed into Haupt's office one day and said: "I have got a thing that will tear up track as quickly as you can say Jack Robinson and spoil the rails so nothing but a rolling mill can ever repair them!" The "thing" was the set of U-shaped iron clamps, held here by the man standing at left, who may be Herman Haupt. Smeed's irons were hooked under a rail, after which wooden levers about 12 feet long were placed in the loop end of the clamp; when men pried down on the handles, the rails were torn free from spikes and chairs holding them to the ties. By using two clamps, a rail could be twisted spirally; the Union officer in this photo is pointing to a section of T-rail that has been ruined by this method. The irons were light and portable, weighing about 6½ pounds, and fence rails could be used as the levers required to serve as handles, making Smeed's invention ideal for use on forays of destruction aimed at enemy railroads.

RAIL REMOVAL

This photograph taken at Alexandria, Virginia, by Capt. A. J. Russell shows a gang of contraband laborers in the act of ripping a rail loose from the ties, using the set of horseshoe-shaped clamps invented by E. C. Smeed. Ropes fastened to the top end of the timbers were used to gain the leverage necessary to pry the rail loose from the spikes holding it to the ties. In the foreground is a section of the old style inverted U type rail, which has been twisted spirally by use of the Smeed clamps.

(Courtesy of the National Archives)

(Courtesy of the National Archives)

RAIL DESTRUCTION

This photograph shows the experiments conducted by General Herman Haupt at Alexandria in his efforts to devise a quick method of destroying rails. Using the Smeed clamps, the colored laborers in the foreground hold a length of U-rail firmly while the gang at the opposite end force it into a spiral twist. The foreman holding the augur may be E. C. Smeed, inventor of the device pictured here. In the background stand two old wooden coaches acquired from the Pennsylvania Railroad by the U.S. Military Railroad.

HEAVY MOTIVE POWER

This photograph taken at Alexandria, Virginia, in July of 1864 shows the E. M. STANTON of the United States Military Railroad; the picture was taken by Capt. A. J. Russell, a skilled photographer, detached from duty with the New York Volunteers to serve as an artist under General Herman Haupt. Many of the views of the Military Railroads and Construction Corps activities appearing in this book are from the glass plates exposed by Captain Russell.

The E. M. STANTON was named in honor of Edwin M. Stanton, Secretary of War in President Lincoln's cabinet; a likeness of the bewhiskered cabinet officer appears on the tank of the locomotive in this photo. It was Stanton who

58

yielded to political pressure and relieved General Herman Haupt from his command of the Construction Corps in 1863, thus robbing the nation of the services of one of the most capable railroad men ever to serve under the Stars and Stripes.

Richard Norris & Son, Philadelphia, Pennsylvania, built the big 4-6-0 shown here on the turntable in 1862 as U.S.M.R.R. HERCULES; her specifications are reported as 18x22 inch cylinders, 48 inch drivers, and a total weight of 59,850 pounds, making her one of the heaviest locomotives on the Military Railroads' roster. Note the roomy cab, with numerous large windows giving it an open-air quality and also exposing the crew to sniper's fire. In a report to General McCallum, Haupt remarked that many of the cabs had been riddled by bullets and the crews forced to lie on the deck of the engine to escape being wounded; he installed boiler-plate linings in the cabs to afford protection to the engine crews.

In the background can be seen part of Haupt's wooden stockade, erected as a defensive measure for the protection of the Alexandria yards and shops. This palisade consisted of logs with their upper ends sharpened in the manner of the frontier log forts used in the Indian wars. The logs were pierced with loopholes at regular intervals for the rifles of the defenders; the steps at the left lead up to an interior parapet or platform designed to permit the defenders to maintain two levels of firepower.

DRESS PARADE

The U.S. Military Railroad engine J. H. DEVEREUX appears here decked with greenery and festoons of decoration for some unrecorded occasion; the drumhead sign on her smokebox door displays an eagle and the motto, "E. Pluribus Unum." In the right background can be seen a portion of another U.S. Military Railroad locomotive, the E. L. WENTZ, a 4-4-0 built by Mason in 1862. This engine was named in honor of Col. E. L. Wentz, who served as a General Superintendent & Chief Engineer on the Military lines in Virginia and later was General Superintendent of U.S. Military Railroads, Division of the Mississippi, with headquarters in Nashville, Tennessee.

In 1872, J. H. Devereux, then General Manager of the Lake Shore & Michigan Southern at Cleveland, Ohio, aided Henry W. Stager and Geo. Myers in the founding of the first Railroad Y.M.C.A.. Stager, a train dispatcher, and Myers, a railroad agent, were granted space in the Cleveland Union Depot by Devereux, who also donated a considerable amount of money to this worthy cause.

(Courtesy of Charles E. Fisher)

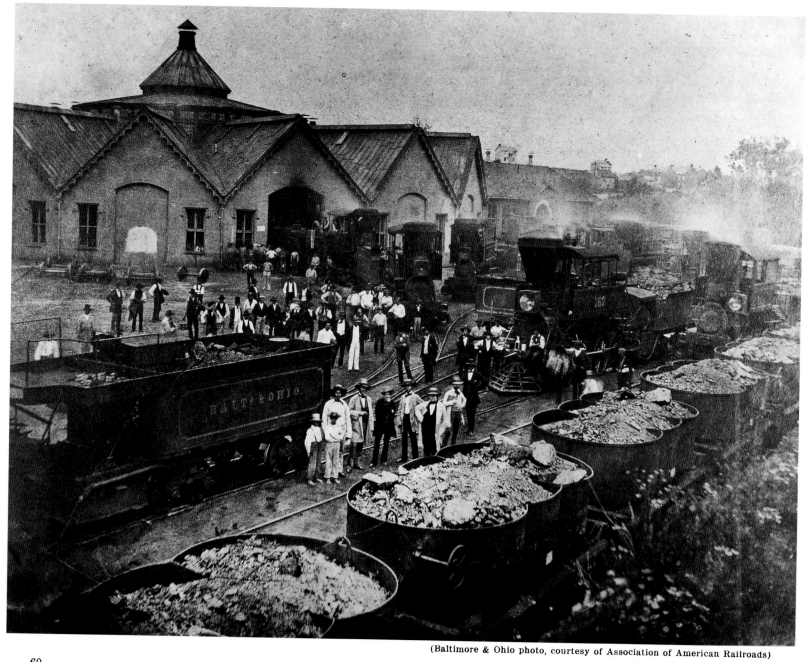

CIVIL WAR TARGET

This war-time view of Martinsburg, in northwestern Virginia, shows the terminal facilities and a number of locomotives of the Baltimore & Ohio Railroad. In the foreground are the old iron "pot" type cars used for transporting coal, forerunners of the modern gondola.

When Confederate forces trapped a large amount of B&O rolling stock in 1861, the Confederate States officials sent Thomas R. Sharp to Martinsburg to supervise the removal of a number of captured locomotives. Sharp was a 27-year old railroader, a Pennsylvanian by birth and an experienced manager of Southern rail lines. He had recently moved two locomotives cross-country from Leesburg, on the Alexandria, Loudon & Hampshire Railroad, to Piedmont Depot on the Manassas Gap Railroad, to prevent them from falling into Union hands.

Sharp gathered a crew of ten teamsters and six machinists, including Hugh Longust, a railroader from Richmond, and 21-year-old locomotive engineer John O'Brien, and set about to move the captured B&O motive power. Using forty horses, Sharp's crew fitted the engines with wooden bogie trucks and moved them along the Shenandoah Valley Turnpike from Martinsburg to Strasburg, Virginia, a distance of forty miles. At Strasburg they had their removed trucks replaced and were set on the rails of the Manassas Gap road to be moved deeper into Confederate territory. Fourteen locomotives were removed in similar fashion from Martinsburg by Sharp and his crew, along with valuable equipment from the B&O shops.

As a sequel to this magnificent undertaking, Sharp moved B&O engine No. 199 from Mount Jackson, the western end of the Manassas Gap road, for a distance of fifty-two miles down the Shenandoah Turnpike to the rails of the Virginia Central R.R. at Staunton, Virginia. This movement, completed in four days, was made in the spring of 1862, after Union forces had sealed off the route to Richmond by occupying Manassas Junction.

Of the 14 engines taken from Martinsburg, 2 were abandoned en route to Strasburg; the B&O recovered 13 of the engines after the War, but the boiler of the other locomotive was placed in a Confederate gun-boat and was lost when the vessel was sunk by the Union Navy.

Thomas Sharp's railroad abilities greatly impressed President John W. Garrett of the B&O, and when the War ended Sharp was employed as a Baltimore & Ohio official, becoming Master of Transportation on the line he had helped to plunder.

INVENTION OF NECESSITY

This photo illustrates a method of connecting rails at a joint without the use of metal angle bars; the ends of two sections of rail are held in line by a length of wooden timber, secured by four bolts. This device was reportedly used by the Confederate railroaders on some of their roads in the South. The scarcity of metal and the Union blockade caused the railroad men operating within the Confederacy to improvise in many ways to keep their trains running.

(Courtesy of the National Archives)

(Courtesy of Chas. E. Fisher)

HONORED RAILROADER

Wm. W. Wright, noted construction supervisor with the United States Military Railroads' Construction Corps, was honored by having a Military Railroad locomotive named after him. This photo shows the engine, W. W. WRIGHT, a 4-4-0 built by the Rogers Locomotive & Machine Works in 1863.

Wright assisted Herman Haupt in the Maryland campaign of 1862, being sent to the Cumberland Valley Railroad, and in December of 1863 he was sent to Tennessee with one division of the Construction Corps (285 men) under Daniel McCallum's command. During the Virginia operations of 1862-63, Wright had been the superintendent and chief engineer of the Aquia Creek operations on the army-controlled portions of the Richmond, Fredericksburg & Potomac Railroad. After some vital repairs on the rail line out of Bridgeport to Chattanooga, Wright was placed on the new rail line being built by the Government from Kingston Springs to Johnsonville, Tennessee. He brought a force of about 2,000 laborers and mechanics from the North to help build this 5 foot gauge pike,

the Nashville & North Western Railroad. The task was completed in less than three months, aided by regiments of Missouri and Michigan engineers and the 12th and 13th Regiments, Colored Infantry.

On February 10th, 1864, McCallum appointed Wright the Chief Engineer of Construction in the western operations. He rebuilt the ravaged Western & Atlantic in the wake of Sherman's march to Atlanta, and then took charge of repairs on the Tennessee & Alabama Railroad line from Nashville to Decatur. Early in 1865 Wright was ordered to take his force to Savannah, Georgia, but the orders were changed en route and the force was sent to Morehead City, North Carolina.

Here Wright was given the task of repairing the Atlantic & North Carolina Railroad. The men landed at Morehead City on February 5th and 6th, 1865, and immediately plunged into the task of restoring the road to operation. By March 30th they had reached the Neuse River, and Wright sent a tracklaying force across the stream to advance the line while the bridge crews rebuilt the missing span. The bridge was completed three days later and on March 25th, the track crews spiked their iron into Goldsboro, North Carolina, at 3:00 A.M. Sherman's army, swinging north on their long trek from Atlanta, had reached Goldsboro the previous day.

Wright had also set to work repairing the Wilmington & Weldon Railroad, and that line was opened into Goldsboro on April 4th, assuring Sherman of two vital supply routes. The story of the victorious struggle up to Appomattox is history, and with the end of the war, the need for the Construction Corps was at an end. On May 15th, 1865, Wright issued the orders to disband his unit and the men were sent to Fortress Monroe, Virginia, to be mustered out. The energy and capability of W. W. Wright was responsible for much of the achievement of the Construction Corps and he deserves a niche in our nation's history for his accomplishments.

more Railroad. The MARYLAND had been built in 1853 by the New Castle Manufacturing Company of New Castle, Delaware, a pioneer firm in business from 1831 to 1857; she had $10\frac{1}{2} \times 16$ inch cylinders, 56 inch drivers, and, at 20,000 pounds, was one of the lightest locomotives on the Military Railroad lines.

The oldest locomotive recorded on the U.S. Military Railroad lines in Virginia was the ROMULUS, a Norris engine built in 1840.

ALEXANDRIA YARD SCENE

This view of the railroad yards was taken from the cupola atop the Orange & Alexandria Railroad roundhouse, looking north; the L-shaped white building at left served as quarters for the "contrabands," the liberated Negro slaves employed by the Construction Corps.

Behind the hospital coaches and freight cars in the foreground are four locomotives used on the U.S. Military Railroads. The engine at right has been tentatively identified as the WASHINGTON, purchased second-hand from the Philadelphia & Reading Railway. She was a Baldwin product of 1846 and bore Shop No. 256; a sister locomotive on the Military Railroads was the INDIANA, Baldwin Shop No. 251, also acquired from the Philadelphia & Reading. These engines had $15\frac{1}{2} \times 20$ inch cylinders and low 46 inch drivers, and weighed 40,000 pounds each. In June of 1862, Supt. J. H. Devereux reported that: "The INDIANA is an old machine, only used as a switching engine in this (Alexandria) yard, poor at that, but has been forced to take part in the Washington work."

The second locomotive from the right is the old MARYLAND, acquired from the Philadelphia, Wilmington & Balti-

BAY STATE NATIVE

This old 4-4-0 with circular steam chests was built by John Souther of Boston in 1854 for the Fitchburg Railroad and was named the HOOSAC. The photograph shown here was copied from an old daguerreotype taken between 1854 and 1862, when the HOOSAC was sold to the Federal Government for service on the United States Military Railroads. Five other Fitchburg Railroad engines were also purchased by the Government for this service. The CHAMPION was one of these, a sister of the HOOSAC, and was built by Souther in 1854. These two locomotives had 16x20 inch cylinders, 56 inch drivers, and weighed 54,000 pounds.

The other four Fitchburg engines were all built by the old New England firm of Hinkley & Drury, a Boston concern that began turning out locomotives about 1841.

The BRATTLEBORO and the LEXINGTON were both constructed in 1844, and bore Shop Numbers 27 and 28; they had 13½x20 inch cylinders and 60 inch drivers, weighing 33,000 pounds each.

Of the two remaining Fitchburg engines, the LINCOLN was built in 1848 under Hinkley & Drury's Shop No. 164; she had 16x20 inch cylinders and 54 inch drivers, tipping the scales at 46,000 pounds. The ONTARIO was also built in 1848, Shop

No. 204; she had 16x20 inch cylinders, 46 inch drivers, and weighed 47,000 pounds.

The LINCOLN and the ONTARIO were captured by the Confederates while in service on the Richmond & York River Railroad, and the LINCOLN may have been destroyed, as no record of her seems to exist after June, 1862. The ONTARIO was in use until the war ended, was reclaimed by the U.S. Government and sold in 1865.

Other U.S. Military Railroad locomotives captured with the LINCOLN and ONTARIO included the WAYANDANK, SPEEDWELL, EXETER, and SPARK. The WAYANDANK was a Baldwin built in 1853 and purchased second-hand from the Long Island Railroad. The SPEEDWELL was built by the Lawrence Machine Works in 1859 and was purchased from the Old Colony & Fall River Railroad. The EXETER was built in 1856 by Hinkley & Drury, and was acquired from the Boston & Maine Railroad, while the SPARK was built by R. Norris & Son in 1862 and was a new locomotive. After her capture by the Confederates, the SPARK was sold to the Raleigh & Gaston Railroad. She was seized by the Federal Government in 1865 and was sold at public auction to the Wilmington & Weldon Railroad, who renamed her ROBER-SON.

NORRIS CREATION

The locomotive pictured here is the GOVERNOR NYE of the United States Military Railroads; she was constructed by the firm of Richard Norris & Son, Philadelphia, in 1863 and bore Norris' Shop No. 1033.

Another Norris engine used by the Military Railroads was the old ROMULUS, an 1840 product probably built in Philadelphia by William Norris. The ROMULUS was owned by the Seaboard & Roanoke Railroad and was captured at Norfolk, Virginia.

The Seaboard & Roanoke Railroad, a standard gauge extending about 80 miles from Portsmouth, Virginia, to Weldon, North Carolina, began to feel the results of the Federal blockade of Southern ports in 1861. Supt. John M. Robinson, later connected with the Confederate Railroad Bureau, reported that the war had shut off his supply of New Bedford whale oil, used extensively as a lubricant, and that the shipments of

Cincinnati-cured bacon used to feed the negroes employed on the road had also been halted. As a remedy for these war-imposed shortages, the Seaboard & Roanoke erected a large smoke house and began to slaughter and cure their own pork; from the refuse of this butchering, they rendered quantities of lard oil which was found to serve admirably as a lubricant, both the bacon and lard oil being obtained at a lower cost than the supplies previously purchased from the North and West.

In the Union advances of 1862, the Federals occupied and used 17 miles of the road between Portsmouth and Suffolk, and later about 14 miles of Seaboard & Roanoke rails were removed for use on other U.S. Military Railroad lines. During the control of the Seaboard & Roanoke and the connecting Norfolk & Petersburg Railroad, the lines were in charge of E. L. Wentz, acting as Superintendent & Engineer for the U.S. Military Railroads.

(Courtesy of National Archives)

BEANPOLES AND CORNSTALKS

Common soldiers of the Army of the Rappahannock, under the command of Major-General Irvin McDowell, were supervised by McDowell's aide-de-camp, Colonel Herman Haupt, in the construction of this noted railroad trestle. The structure was erected at the site of a destroyed span of the Richmond, Fredericksburg & Potomac Railroad over Potomac Creek, Virginia. The trestle was built in nine working days in May of 1862, and contained more than two million feet of lumber, most of it cut from woodlands near the site. The soldiers working under Haupt's direction were poorly equipped, lacked proper tools, were hampered by wet weather, and their rations were scant, but the job they accomplished excited a high degree of wonder and admiration, especially from the European officers who had come to witness the Civil War.

In his defense before a Court of Inquiry, Major-General McDowell made the following statement regarding the trestle: "It is a structure which ignores all the rules and precedents of military science as laid down in the books. It is constructed chiefly of round sticks cut from the woods, and not even divested of bark; the legs of the trestles are braced with round poles. It is in four stories, three of trestle and one of crib work. The total height from the deepest part of the stream to the rail is nearly 80 feet. It carries daily from 10 to 20 heavy railway trains in both directions, and has withstood several severe freshets and storms without injury."

After a visit to McDowell's headquarters, President Lincoln remarked in awe that "That man Haupt has built a bridge across Potomac Creek, about 400 feet long . . . and, upon my word, gentlemen, there is nothing in it but beanpoles and cornstalks."

The Richmond, Fredericksburg & Potomac rail line from Aquia Creek to Fredericksburg was used to supply the Union forces in that area and the flow of traffic was very heavy. When the troops commanded by Major-General Ambrose E. Burnside, who had replaced McDowell, retreated after the battle of Fredericksburg in December, 1862, the noted Potomac Creek trestle was destroyed by them to stall the Confederate pursuit. Colonel Haupt had vigorously opposed the destruction, terming it an act of vandalism on the part of the Federal troops. When the Union forces gained control of the line after Antietam, a more substantial bridge was erected to replace the destroyed timber trestle.

———•———

TRESTLE APPROACH

The tracks of the Richmond, Fredericksburg & Potomac Railroad passed through a deep cut and swung around the curve shown here in their approach to the famous "bean-pole and corn-stalk" trestle across Potomac Run. On the gentle rise beyond the deep ravine can be seen the rows of white tents of an encampment of Federal forces. Much of the growth of timber in the immediate vicinity had been cut to furnish the material used in erecting the high trestle.

(Courtesy of National Archives)

(Courtesy of the Southern Railway)

CAPITOL SECURITY

When the Confederate troops moved into the northern portion of Virginia in 1863, the Federal forces feared a loss of their valuable rolling stock and precautionary measures were taken. In his report filed in 1866, Col. D. C. McCallum, the General Manager of the United States Military Railroads, remarked: "In April, 1863, the Orange & Alexandria railroad was opened to Bealeton, and used a few days to supply a force on the Rappahannock. The portion south of Bull Run was then abandoned, and on about the 15th of June the whole road outside the defenses of Washington was evacuated." This photograph was probably taken shortly after, and shows at least 17 locomotives stored under the shadow of the dome of the National Capitol building in Washington, D.C. The engine in the right foreground is unidentified; on the track ahead of it is the COL. A. BECKWITH (ex-P. H. WATSON), a Norris 4-4-0 received in 1863. The next engine in line is unidentified, but directly ahead of it is the COMMODORE, a New Jersey Loco. Works product, then the FIREFLY, a Norris 4-4-0, and the EAGLE, another New Jersey Locomotive & Machine Works product built in 1862.

The locomotive beyond the crossing on the spur track at the left is probably the VULCAN, a Baldwin 4-4-0 built in 1862.

The Alexandria & Washington road, 7 miles long, connected the capital with the big Military Railroad terminal located on the Orange & Alexandria Railroad at Alexandria, Virginia. This terminal was the scene of much railroad activity during the various campaigns throughout the war, with three rail lines terminating there.

POTOMAC RIVER CROSSING

These two views show the Long Bridge across the Potomac River at Washington, D.C. The bridge was over 5,000 feet long and was the sole railroad connection between the National Capital and the important rail junction of Alexandria, Virginia. The view showing the wooden through truss was taken on the Virginia end of the span; the view of the Washington end shows three men seated on a track gang's push car, the hatless, bearded man in the center probably being General D. C. McCallum.

(Both photos, courtesy of the National Archives)

A DARING CREW

In the autumn of 1861 the main line of the Baltimore & Ohio Railroad was occupied by Confederate raiders below Harper's Ferry, Virginia, and all through train movements were halted. However, before the rebels took possession of the line a special train consisting of a locomotive and one coach had passed the site of the raid and was headed west for Wheeling This special was fired upon by a couple of guerrillas while passing through the section known as Black Oak Bottom, but their aim was erratic and no harm was done. When the special pulled up at Oakland, Maryland, to refuel and take water, word was received by telegraph that a rebel force was hurrying toward the line west of there, evidently intending to try to capture the special, which was carrying several Northern notables. While engaged in taking fuel and water at Oakland, the fireman had the misfortune to fall and break an arm, but a former B&O engineer present volunteered to take his place and the train roared out of town. Travelling at high speed, the special approached the deep gorge near the Cheat River bridge and as it swept round a curve, the crew spied a group of gray-clad men engaged in prying up a rail and others were busily piling logs and ties across the track. Here the lack of railroad knowledge lost the day for the Confederates, for in their ignorance they had removed the rail from the inside of the curve. The runner jerked his throttle wide and the gallant engine pounded across the bare ties and mounted the rail beyond the break; the volunteer fireman expertly sent a stick of firewood flying into the huddled raiders, up-ending several of them. The brave runner who had stuck to his throttle throughout the exciting dash mounted the cab roof, produced a pocket flask, and after a mocking bow to the chagrined raiders, coolly proceeded to take a drink. The enraged "rebs" fired a ragged volley after the escaped train without causing any damage. When out of range, although still within sight of the frustrated train wreckers, the special was braked to a halt to permit an examination of the locomotive. The force of the collision with the ties and poles obstructing the track had broken the pilot badly, smashed the big oil headlight, and dented the smokebox and cylinder casings, but the damage was minor and the train was soon speeding west to its destination in Wheeling.

The engineer who had saved the day and demonstrated his lack of fear of the enemy's marksmanship met his death in an engine cab later in the war, being shot and killed while running a locomotive for the Military Railroad near Chattanooga, Tennessee.

Baltimore & Ohio's No. 201, shown here, was an inside-connected 4-4-0 and a typical engine in use on the road during the stirring days of the Rebellion.

B. & O. MOTIVE POWER

Engine No. 17 of the Baltimore & Ohio Railroad is pictured here on the approach to the bridge at Harper's Ferry. The photograph was probably taken about 1860. The American Railroad Journal, a contemporary publication of Civil War days, reported that between May of 1861 and March of 1862, the Baltimore & Ohio had 42 locomotives damaged or destroyed as a result of the War.

(Courtesy of Leonard W. Rice, Railroadographs)

72

VIRGINIA PILE-UP

The engine COMMODORE of the United States Military Railroads is pictured here after having been derailed by Confederates in one of the campaigns in northern Virginia. In the background a track gang labors to restore the main line at the scene of the wreck, for the traffic must continue to move; the overturned locomotive and cars will be recovered later when the flow of military traffic has been restored.

The COMMODORE and a sister engine, the CHAS. MINOT, were both built by the New Jersey Locomotive & Machine Co. in 1863.

The time book of a conductor on the Military Railroad, now in the hands of Pres. Chas. E. Fisher of the Railway & Locomotive Historical Society, mentions a trip behind the MINOT in 1863. The train left Alexandria at 6:10 on November 5th and reached Warrenton Junction on the Orange & Alexandria R.R. at 10:25; her consist included 4 cars of oats, 5 cars of ordnance stores, 2 cars of lumber, and 2 cars of construction material for Supt. Devereux. On the return trip, the MINOT left Warrenton Junction at 6:05 with 15 empty cars and arrived in Alexandria at 9:35.

This same time book records many other trips made by Conductor John M. Lydecker, including one made in October of 1863 behind the locomotive STUART GWYNN with Engineer James E. Johnson, Fireman John M. Johnson, and Brakemen Kelsey and Jennings. On November 21st, Condr. Lydecker left Alexandria with 12 cars loaded with horses, hauled by Engr. Jenks and the USMRR engine E. CORNING. The train ran as an extra to Bealton, where the horses were unloaded; the crew picked up 4 empty cars at Bealton and departed at 8:25 with the total of 16 empties, reaching the Alexandria terminal at 12:53 (no A.M. or P.M. is given in the conductor's book for the times shown).

The train order for the return trip has been preserved:

Bealton Nov. 21st, 1863

Condr. & Engr.

Eng. CORNING, 2nd Ex. No. 8.

Follow red signals on Eng. WRIGHT to Alexandria as 2nd extra No. 8.

J.H.D.

The initials, J.H.D., on the above copy of this old order are those of Supt. John H. Devereux. On a trip made between Alexandria and Brandy early in January, 1864, Condr. Lydecker rode behind the Military Railroad engine ZEBRA, with Engineer Beattie at the throttle; other railroaders who worked with Lydecker in Virginia include Engr. Furguson, Fireman Magruder, and Brakemen W. W. Jennings, James Wolcott, Kelsey, and Mitchell.

CLEANING UP WRECKAGE

Employees of the U.S. Military Railroad are depicted here in the act of clearing debris from the track after a train wreck on the Alexandria, Loudon & Hampshire Railroad in Virginia. Although the wrecking train has a hand-powered crane on the flat car behind the caboose, the men are loading car wheels mounted on axles by rolling them up a wooden ramp by hand, while officers and members of the train crew look on. The broken car trucks are probably destined for the repair shops located in Alexandria.

(Courtesy of the National Archives)

PROUD EIGHTWHEELER

This lovely 4-4-0 was built for the United States Military Railroads in 1862 by William Mason in his machine works located in Taunton, Massachusetts. The engine was named the W. H. WHITON and bore Mason's shop number 113. She was delivered to the Military Railroad at Alexandria, Virginia, on July 21st, 1862. Mason records reportedly state that she was the first of a number of locomotives built by them for the United States Government for use in the Civil War. Although no definite record has been established, this view of the standard gauge beauty was probably taken on the long bridge over the Potomac River, linking Washington, D.C., with Alexandria, Virginia. The engine had 15x22 inch cylinders, 60 inch driving wheels, and weighed 55,000 pounds. At the close of the war she was sold to the Baltimore & Ohio Railroad for $15,450.

To add to the confusion of those who attempt to trace the history of old motive power, the United States Military Railroads received a second locomotive on July 29th, 1862, that bore the same name, W. H. WHITON. This engine was built by R. Norris & Son in 1862 and was sent by the Government to Columbus, Kentucky. The Norris engine had 16x24 inch cylinders, 56 inch drivers, and weighed 57,910 pounds. Other Norris-built locomotives of 1862 that appear on the U.S. Military Railroads' roster included the MADISON, MONROE, JEFFERSON, and WASHINGTON, all constructed on the same dimensions as the W. H. WHITON.

Columbus, Kentucky, was the northern terminus of the 5 foot gauge Mobile & Ohio Railroad, first of the land grant roads. The line from Mobile, Alabama, to Columbus was 472 miles long and was opened for service in 1859, construction having been started in 1849.

IRON HORSE STABLE

This view shows the multi-stalled roundhouse of the Orange & Alexandria Railroad located in Alexandria, Virginia, during the Civil War years while it was used by the U.S. Military Railroad. The big structure formed a complete circle, with a turntable in the center, covered by the cupola-topped roof. When a strike on the Philadelphia & Reading Railroad tied up shipments of coal needed for the Federal Navy in July of 1864, General D. C. McCallum sent train and engine crews from the Military Railroad in Alexandria to operate the road. The strike lasted two weeks, after which the Alexandria crews were returned to their military duties. The Military Railroad operations of the Orange & Alexandria Railroad ended on June 27th, 1865, when the road was turned over to the Virginia Board of Public Works.

(Courtesy of the National Archives)

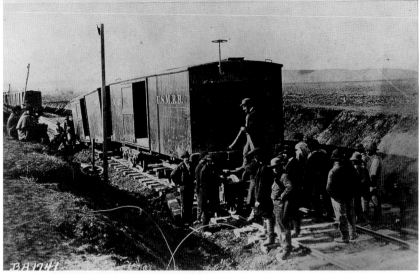

OPERATIONAL HAZARD

This pile-up reportedly occurred on the Alexandria, Loudon & Hampshire Railroad on March 28, 1863, and was caused by the broken axle visible just beyond the telegraph pole in the left foreground. The box car bears the initials of the United States Military Railroad. The Alexandria, Loudon & Hampshire Railroad was chartered in 1853 and the 38 miles of standard gauge track was opened to Leesburg, Virginia, in the summer of 1858.

The 15 miles of track of the Alexandria, Loudon &Hampshire extending from Alexandria to Vienna, Virginia, was

placed under Federal operations in the spring of 1862 and the road played a vital role in transporting supplies to the ring of Army camps and fortifications thrown up along the line for the defense of Washington, D.C.

After the Gettysburg fight in 1863, the Union forces under General Meade followed the retreating troops of General Robert E. Lee into northern Virginia and a number of minor engagements took place, including Culpeper Court House, Raccoon Ford, and Kelly's Ford. Early in September, after the second battle of Bull Run, the Army of the Potomac went into camp near Washington and the Alexandria, Loudon & Hampshire served as the principal supply line for the large concentration of troops encamped along the south bank of the Potomac.

SHERMAN'S NECKTIES

This photograph clearly depicts the most common method of destroying rails during the Civil War. Task forces pulled the spikes and removed the light iron rails, then gathered the hand-hewn ties into piles and laid the sections of rail across them. The ties were then fired and the burning wood heated the center sections of the soft metal, the weight of the unsupported ends causing the rails to droop and bend out of shape. If time permitted, raiders bent upon destroying track by this method frequently grasped the cooler outer ends of these heated rails and wrapped them around the nearest convenient tree trunk; this method was used frequently by Sherman's troops on their march through Georgia, and the twisted iron left in their wake was nick-named "Sherman's neckties."

The Construction Corps of the Union Army also devised a U-shaped iron device for twisting rails and rendering them unfit for use. Not all of the rail in use on captured lines met this fate; if time and transportation facilities permitted, the rails were frequently hauled away for use by the captors on other railways, and only the ties were consigned to the destructive flames. When Confederate forces retired from Aquia Creek, Virginia, in 1862, they tore up about three miles of track of the Richmond, Fredericksburg & Potomac Railroad, carrying away the rails and burning the ties and wooden bridges. Even the roadbed in their wake suffered, being cut up by cavalry troops and wagon trains moving along it.

MARYLAND MOTIVE POWER

This photo shows the locomotive JOHN M. FORBES of the Philadelphia, Wilmington & Baltimore Railroad, a 4-4-0 built by Baldwin in 1861, Shop No. 993.

President-elect Abraham Lincoln arrived aboard a PW&B train in Baltimore in February, 1861, on his way to Washington for his inauguration. Rumors that an attempt would be made on Lincoln's life caused President Felton to arm 200 men and post them as guards along the line; whispered stories that the Back River bridge on the road would be burned caused Felton to have the structure white-washed with a mixture of alum and salt in an effort to make the wooden span fireproof.

On the 19th of April, 1861, 35 cars loaded with about 2,000 troops arrived at the President Street Station of the PW&B and a transfer movement, one car at a time, started along Pratt Street to the B&O's Camden station, about one mile distant. A mob of Southern sympathizers gathered and began to harass the troops; when a car broke and had to be returned to President Street, the occupants, members of the 6th Massachusetts Regiment commanded by Colonel Edward F. Jones, began to march to the B&O transfer point. Although Mayor Brown, Chief of Police Kane, and 50 city police escorted the troopers, the mob became more violent and firing broke out as the soldiers neared Commerce Street. When the smoke cleared, 4 soldiers and 12 civilians were dead, 36 soldiers and an uncounted number of civilians wounded, and the city in a great turmoil. In a meeting held on the night of April 19th, Governor Hicks, ex-Governor Lowe, Mayor Brown, and Chief of Police Kane decided to prevent a recurrence of the riots by cutting the rail lines leading north from Baltimore. Task forces composed of the Purnell Legion of Maryland, headed by Lt. Col. Johnson and 1st Lt. Hubbell, burned three bridges on the PW&B and three on the Northern Central. It was not until May 14th that service on the PW&B was restored.

(Baldwin Loco. Wks. negative, courtesy of H. L. Broadbelt)

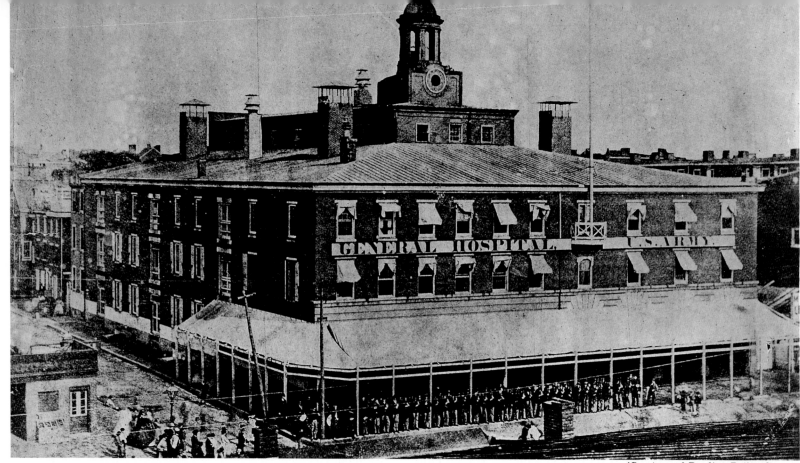

HAVEN OF MERCY

The Civil War took a terrible toll of human life, the Union forces losing over 395,000 men and the Confederates losing about 258,000. Added to the thousands who were wounded in battle were those who fell ill or were otherwise injured in their daily duties. Field hospitals were swamped following big battles and the lack of proper medical attention contributed to the frightful loss of life. As the war progressed, better sanitary facilities were provided and the increased use of the railroads for transporting the wounded away from the actual battlefields to hospitals in the North lessened some of the loss and suffering.

This photograph, taken in 1862, shows a General Hospital of the United States Army with a file of armed troops lined up in front of it. The building was the former depot of the Philadelphia, Reading & Pottsville Railroad and was located at the southeast corner of Broad and Cherry Streets in Philadelphia, Pennsylvania. The old station, built about 1838, was first opened as a military hospital in December of 1861; it provided accommodations for 650 patients.

As the flow of wounded increased many other military hospitals capable of holding larger numbers of patients were set up in various parts of Philadelphia as well as in other Northern cities.

Hospital cars were first introduced by the North in 1862 to aid in evacuating wounded soldiers from the battlefields. Before the carnage was ended, over 225,000 wounded men were moved over the rails in the cars equipped for this service.

ROLLING STOCK

This view of the United States Military Railroad was taken in Alexandria, Virginia, and depicts a wide variety of rail equipment, including locomotives, box cars, stock car, passenger coaches, and a hospital car. An early recorded use of hospital cars was in the fall of 1862 when the Sanitary Commission placed two converted cars in operation on a branch of the Louisville & Nashville after the battle of Perryville. The success of this method of moving wounded led the Commission to design a regular car for hospital service. Built with strong springs and cushioned draft gear, these cars had upright interior posts from which 24 stretchers could be suspended by heavy rubber bands. Wounded were thus able to be loaded on field stretchers, conveyed to the car and placed in these hanging, flexible supports. Upon arrival at terminals where hospital facilities were available, the stretchers and occupants could be removed at once and the car could be returned for further use. These cars also contained a small kitchen area, water tank, a boiler, and facilities for surgeons. Their improved ventilation, lighting, and heating made them a great deal more comfortable than the box cars that had formerly been pressed into service to transport wounded soldiers, the victims being simply laid on a thin covering of straw on the freight car floors with scant attention to comfort or sanitary conditions.

The Army medical department and the Sanitary Commission had charge of the hospital cars; most of them were paid for by the Government, although the Sanitary Commission spent over $9,000 on them. Despite these efforts, there were never enough hospital cars to meet the demand, and makeshift equipment had to be pressed into service, especially after major battles.

Hospital trains ran in all of the theaters of war and the wounded were carried into New England from the various battlefields along the eastern seaboard, being routed from Washington to Boston via New York and Springfield. A typical hospital train consist in the Western Theater of operations included a wood-burning locomotive, 5 ward cars, a surgeon's car, a cook car, a dispensary car, a passenger coach, and a caboose. The coach was customarily used for wounded who were able to sit up, but the seats could be altered into beds if required. These trains were distinctively marked and the Confederates respected their neutrality with only a few minor exceptions. An old drawing shows one such brigade of cars lettered "HOSPITAL TRAIN," drawn by the engine FRANK THOMPSON.

(Courtesy of Southern Railway)

ARTILLERY VICTIM

This photograph clearly depicts the accuracy of Confederate artillery in use during the Civil War. The man standing on the rear sill of the tank at right is pointing to a neat hole drilled into the flare-board of the tender, while the man at far left, standing on the pilot beam, points out the riddled funnel stack. The United States Military Railroads locomotive is the FRED LEACH, a 4-4-0 built by the New Jersey Locomotive & Machine Works in 1862. In addition to the holes blown in her stack and tank, the LEACH has her rear steam dome cover knocked askew, and the photo shows the left main rod taken down. The damage was inflicted on August 1st, 1863, as the locomotive was running along the tracks of the Orange & Alexandria Railroad near Union Mills, Virginia. The FRED LEACH was repaired and after the war was over she was sold by the Federal Government to the Orange & Alexandria Railroad for $15,000; the O & A renamed this engine the WARRENTON, after the town located at the western terminus of the Warrenton branch. The engine was built with 16x24 inch cylinders and 56 inch drivers. Other New Jersey Locomotive & Machine Works engines in use on the U.S. Military Railroads in Virginia included the J. H. DEVEREUX, the COL. McCALLUM, and the GOVERNMENT.

The fortunes of war swept over the Orange & Alexandria throughout most of the conflict, and the line and equipment used on it often changed hands. When Union Army forces under General Pope were forced into retreat in the last days of August, 1862, seven locomotives and two hundred and ninety-five cars fell into the hands of the advancing Confederates.

WOODEN GUARDIAN

This United States Military Railroad truss bridge is guarded by the wooden blockhouse standing on the knoll above the track at right. These forts, constructed in the style used on the frontier for defense against Indians, were garrisoned with soldiers in an attempt to prevent damage by raiding parties of Confederates and guerrillas. Haupt stated that the Prince William Cavalry raided the Federal rail lines and that other damage was inflicted by John S. Mosby's men, described by Haupt as: "... guerrillas by night and farmers by day." Some of the railroad bridges guarded by troops in Virginia in 1862 included those at Accotink, Bull Run, Springfield, and near Burke's Station.

(Courtesy of the National Archives)

(National Archives photo, courtesy Southern Ry).

GANDY DANCERS AT WAR

When Herman Haupt was appointed chief of construction and transportation early in May of 1862, he set about organizing a force of laborers to rebuild, repair, and construct the railroad lines used by the Federal forces in their military campaigns. Although soldiers were at first detailed to this work, Haupt gradually built up a corps of hired civilians, including numbers of contraband negroes, former slaves liberated by the Union Army's advances. By June of 1862 this force had a strength of about 300 men, divided into 10-man squads. An officer was placed in charge of two squads, the foremen being equal in rank to Army lieutenants, and each civilian superintendent carried the equivalent rank of an Army captain. The Construction Corps gathered a supply of tools necessary for track work, and also had a number of yoke of oxen for moving their equipment, clearing heavy debris, etc.

Soon the Corps was enlarged to include a bridge-building department, and eventually the outfit was engaged in constructing freight cars, barracks, wharves, warehouses, enginehouses, and all of the other adjuncts of a railroad operating in a war zone.

Originally organized in Virginia, the activities of the Corps extended to Tennessee in 1863 and the force accomplished many feats of skill in restoring rail operations in that shattered region. Sherman's thrust through Georgia was heavily dependent upon the work of the Corps in opening and maintaining his supply lines.

The men worked long hours, day and night, and were frequently exposed to rebel fire as they struggled to keep the tracks in repair.

This view was taken along the Orange & Alexandria Railroad in Fauquier County, Virginia, and shows the squads of laborers clearing debris and repairing track after a raid.

SALVAGE JOB

The workmen shown here are in the process of righting the overturned locomotive CHAS. MINOT of the United States Military Railroads, a 4-4-0 built by the New Jersey Locomotive & Machine Co. in 1863. Blocks rigged with rope were commonly used to hoist cars and engines into position for re-railing. Confederate troops on raids behind Northern lines frequently left such scenes behind them, while other wrecks were caused by bands of roving guerrillas.

When the Manassas Gap Railroad to Piedmont, Virginia, was being repaired in October of 1864, guerrillas wrecked a

train and cost the lives of Supt. M. J. McCrickett and four other Military Railroad men. McCrickett, a veteran of the U.S. Military Railroad service, was riding one of the engines double-heading a train over the road. Guerrillas had removed all the spikes from a section of rail, but left the rail in place in the track so that nothing appeared wrong to the sharp eyes of the engineers; as the two woodburners thundered up, the raiders jerked the rail out of the track by means of a length of telegraph wire leading to it from their place of concealment in a brushy thicket. Both engines hurtled down a steep embankment, killing McCrickett and the four crewmen. A fitting tribute to these brave men who died at their posts appeared in a Special Order of E. L. Wentz, General Supt. of Military Railroads in Virginia, dated October 11th, 1864:

"The unfortunate victims of this latest atrocity were faithful and valuable public servants—men who, knowing the danger incident to their duty, fearlessly encountered it, and lost their lives executing the trust reposed in them. Though not equipped with the implements of war and sent upon the battlefield where fame is won, they have none the less sacrificed their lives upon the sacred altar of our country, and de-serve a place in our memories among the honored dead who have fallen in its defense."

On the 10th of April, 1863, a locomotive engineer on the Norfolk & Petersburg Railroad failed to comply with instructions and his locomotive plunged through the open draw of the bridge over the South Fork of the Elizabeth River. The engine was badly damaged, four cars destroyed, and Capt. J. B. Bowdisa, Commissary of Subsistence at Suffolk who was riding the engine, was killed.

The Military Railroad had taken over the Norfolk & Petersburg on July 22nd, 1862, and reduced the gauge from 5 feet to 4 feet, 8½ inches from Norfolk to within a mile of the Blackwater River, a distance of 44 miles. In addition, a mile of track was laid at Suffolk to connect with the Seaboard & Roanoke Railroad; the N&P shops in Petersburg were in Confederate hands and equipment had to be repaired in the Seaboard & Roanoke shops located in Portsmouth. Military Railroad officers on these joint roads in 1862-63 included E. L. Wentz, Supt. Engr.; J. McCallum, Asst. Supt.; C. L. McAlpine, Asst. Engr.; and Mr. William Cessford, Master Mechanic.

84

PROUD CREW

The two men shown here with the GENL. HAUPT in the Alexandria yards could be justly proud of their polished wood-burner, for she had the graceful lines that typified William Mason's locomotives.

The man whose name she bore spared no efforts to keep his tracks clear for the movement of his trains and devoted his energy to protecting his crews and equipment. In a message sent from Alexandria to General Rufus King at Centreville, Virginia, in July of 1863, Herman Haupt detailed some of his activities:

"Yesterday morning, on returning from a reconnoissance to White Plains, I passed the western-bound train at Burkes' about 5 A.M. Conductor reported that his train had been fired into at Accotink, eight miles from Alexandria. As I had no train guard with me, I returned to Fairfax, procured two companies, and scoured the woods about Accotink, but found no enemy. Fresh horse tracks, however, were numerous. I learn this morning that before the train passed rails had been taken out and obstructions placed upon the track by these guerrillas, but some of the track men had seen and repaired the damage. These men are supposed to be part of Mosby's gang. I heard of them the evening on which I was over the Gap road as being at Wolf Run Shoals, and I also heard of the proximity of Mosby's men at Thoroughfare and other points.

"To enable us to operate the road with any security, we must have cavalry pickets along the Occoquan and at the Gaps of the Blue Ridge; also patrols through the country. Every citizen of suitable age for draft, who is not in the army, should be regarded with suspicion and closely watched, for I am told that many of them have been exempted from draft on condition of joining Mosby's band, who are guerrillas by night and farmers by day. Our trains will be run as much as possible by daylight and with train guards, but with a heavy business we cannot avoid running at night, and train guards afford but little protection."

Haupt was probably correct in assuming that the raids on his precious rail lines were led by John Singleton Mosby. That daring raider and his band of Rangers harassed the Union forces in Virginia with a series of audacious incidents; in March of 1863, Mosby and a small group numbering about 29 men slipped through the heart of a heavy concentration of Federal forces and entered Fairfax, Virginia. Mosby and his Rangers located the billet of the Union commander, Brigadier General Edwin Stoughton, kidnapped him, and escaped with their prize catch, along with a number of other captured Yankees and some sorely-needed horses.

POTOMAC PLUNGER

In March of 1864 the engine C. VIBBARD of the U.S. Military Railroad fell through a span of the Long Bridge over the Potomac River at Washington, D.C.; the locomotive was fished out of the river with blocks and tackle suspended from a wooden frame erected overhead at the site of her dunking. The C. VIBBARD, pictured here, was built by Baldwin in 1862 under Shop No. 1097. As in all wars, profiteering marked our civil strife; both civilian and military railroads complained of poor equipment, engines received with tools left in the boilers, etc. The Military Railroad was displeased with cars built by the A. L. Mowry firm, reportedly constructed with loose wheels and weak springs which caused operating accidents. In return, contractors complained of red tape and slow pay on the part of the Quartermaster Dept.; the Cambria Iron Works had difficulty in collecting monies owed them, and Military Railroad employees were forced to wait for long periods before cashing their pay vouchers.

(Courtesy of Ansco Brady collection)

MILITARY RAILROAD YARDS

These four views show the tracks used by the U.S. Military Railroads at three Virginia railroad stations during the Civil War. The upper view is the terminal facilities and roundhouse on the Orange & Alexandria Railroad in Alexandria, showing box cars, coaches, and some flat cars loaded with forage. At center is a view of the yards at Manchester, Virginia, showing the stone piers of a destroyed railroad bridge in the left background. The lower left photo is a view of Stoneman's Station, showing the huge piles of stores accumulated for use by the Union armies. The lower right photo shows troops and cars at Catlet's Station on the Orange & Alexandria Railroad.

When the Military Railroad crews first moved into Fredericksburg, Virginia, friendly Negroes pointed out a number of mines the retreating Rebels had planted under the yard tracks. These were carefully removed and the first train was made up with a flat car load of scrap in front and the engine behind the cars, in case any of the mines had been overlooked. The mines were stored in a shed near the yards and a sentry placed on guard there. He evidently tinkered with one, and the resulting blast shook the town; no trace of the guard could be located.

(Upper, courtesy of Ansco Brady collection)
(Center and lower, courtesy of National Archives)

(Courtesy of Southern Railway)

HOME FOR REPAIRS

This photograph shows members of the Military Railroad corps ready to return to Alexandria, Virginia, with the salvaged equipment picked up after a wreck caused by the Confederates. The big 4-6-0 at the right is the RAPIDAN, a confiscated Orange & Alexandria Railroad locomotive built in 1856 at Alexandria, Virginia. She was a product of the Virginia Locomotive & Car Works, formerly known as Smith & Perkins. She had 16x20 inch cylinders, 50 inch drivers, and weighed 55,000 pounds. In 1883 she became No. 5 of the Washington City, Virginia Midland & Great Southern Railroad, a company formed by consolidation of the former Orange & Alexandria, the Manassas Gap, and the Lynchburg & Danville railroads. In 1884 she became Virginia Midland's No. 27.

Coupled behind the RAPIDAN is the wrecked equipment that had been sent crashing down an embankment. The salvaged engines and tenders were both U.S. Military Railroad locomotives, one being the COMMODORE and the other the UNION. The COMMODORE was built by New Jersey Locomotive & Machine Works and was received by the Military Railroad on May 16, 1863. She had 16x24 inch cylinders and 60 inch drivers. When hostilities ended, the Government sold her to the Wilmington & Weldon Railroad for $15,000; she was later transferred to the Orange & Alexandria and renamed VIRGINIA.

The UNION was a 4-4-0 built by Baldwin in June, 1862, under Shop No. 1061. Her specifications included 16x24 inch cylinders and 54 inch drivers. The UNION was one of the locomotives sent to North Carolina during the campaign there in 1865, and when the war ended she was sold to the Baltimore & Ohio Railroad. When this photo was taken, the RAPIDAN was moving the wrecked engines to the Alexandria shops to be repaired.

87

METAL TREASURE

(U.S. Signal Corps photo, Courtesy of National Archives)

The vast stores of rail shown here in the U.S. Military Railroad yards in Alexandria would have been worth a king's ransom in the Confederacy. Iron rails were in general use when the War broke out and some Southern roads were still using wooden stringers faced with strap iron. The heavy flow of wartime traffic caused the soft iron to wear badly and the Yankee blockade prevented the South from importing new supplies in any quantity. Some of the lines had small stockpiles on hand when the War started, but the Confederate Navy seized many of the priceless bars for armoring their famous iron-clad vessels. Attempts to confiscate the rails of unimportant lines in the South were met with violent objections and threats of open rebellion against the newly-formed Confederate Government.

The industrial North, with extensive iron deposits and manufacturing facilities, was in a far better position to meet the demand for rails and other metal products used by the railroads. General McCallum's report of 1866 stated that 21,783 tons of rails had been purchased for the Military Railroads between 1862 and 1865. In addition, the Government had torn up the rails of some Southern roads for use elsewhere, including 35 miles of the Manassas Gap line, 41 miles of the Winchester & Fayetteville, and 26 miles of the McMinnville & Manchester.

LUMBER SUPPLY POINT

This photograph shows the United States Military Railroad lumber yard at Alexandria, Virginia, in April of 1864. The men of the Construction Corps used large quantities of timber in bridge and trestle work, wharves, and other structures built by them. Finished lumber also went into the repair and construction of railroad cars in the Military Railroad car shops. From the stores of lumber gathered by the Military Railroad in Virginia quantities were shipped to points where it was sorely needed; material for bridging was hurriedly sent to the short lines serving the Army in Pennsylvania during the Gettysburg campaign, and other shipments were furnished to the Baltimore & Ohio Railroad for use in replacing destroyed bridges.

Records indicate that the Military Railroads had difficulty in securing timber from land-owners in the various Depart-ments; vast amounts were needed for ties, locomotive fuel, and other uses. One Government lumber inspector was discharged from the Construction Corps for dishonesty, after attempting to bribe a lumber contractor. The crooked inspector had offered, for a fee, to alter his books and show the receipt of a large amount of lumber which had never been delivered.

Behind the two men standing at left in this photo can be seen a number of push cars marked "U.S.M.R.R.," while on top of the pile of timbers behind them rests an early track car used by track men; instead of the familiar handles pumped by men facing each other, this vehicle was propelled by turning a set of cranks.

On top of the pile of lumber in the right foreground appears the top or bottom of one of the old style of coffins in use at the time, called the "pinch toe" model.

(Courtesy of Ansco Brady collection)

(Courtesy of Dr. S. R. Wood)

TAUNTON WORKS PRODUCT

The Taunton Locomotive Works, located in Taunton, Massachusetts, operated from about 1847 to 1889, and turned out many fine locomotives. Pictured here at the Taunton factory is the STUART GWYNN, built in 1863 for the United States Military Railroads. She was a 4-4-0 bearing Taunton's Shop No. 297, and sported 16x24 inch cylinders and 60 inch drivers; her total weight was listed as being 56,000 pounds.

Other Taunton locomotives used by the U.S. Military Railroads in Virginia and North Carolina included the CHIEF, built in 1862, and the GRAPESHOT, E. CORNING, SECRETARY, and GENL. COUCH, all built in 1863. When the war ended, the E. CORNING was sold to the Central Ohio Railroad for $15,000. The engines GRAPESHOT and SECRETARY were sold to the North Carolina Railroad, along with the

LION, a New Jersey Loco. & Machine Works product, and another U.S. Military Railroad engine named the COL. WEBSTER.

Taunton also built about 15 numbered locomotives used by the U.S. Military Railroads in Tennessee and Mississippi, most of them constructed in 1864-65.

With the ending of the war, the Nashville & Decatur Railroad purchased at least one Taunton-built engine from the Military Railroads, No. 181. A 4-4-0 built in 1864, she carried Taunton Shop No. 324, became Nashville & Decatur's No. 17 and later became Louisville & Nashville's No. 317. R. E. Prince, noted authority on L&N power, states that the Nashville & Decatur acquired a number of other locomotives from the U.S. Military Railroads which had been brought south during the war.

90

ROUGH BUT READY

Construction Corps personnel erected this rude trestle over Hatcher's Run, Virginia. The trestle was 1,240 feet long and composed mainly of trees cut from the nearby stands of timber; note the stumps in the foreground. It was in the vicinity of Hatcher's Run that Union forces under Sheridan captured some 5,000 Confederates in the last of March, 1865, shortly before the fall of Petersburg.

(Virginia Historical Society photo, courtesy of National Archives)

REPLACEMENT SPAN

This military truss bridge was erected under the direction of General Haupt to replace the old "beanpole and cornstalk" bridge over Potomac Creek on the Richmond, Fredericksburg & Potomac Railroad. Completed early in 1863, the new truss bridge was installed without delaying a single train, although traffic over the road was heavy during its construction.

(Virginia Historical Society photo, courtesy of National Archives)

(Courtesy of the Association of American Railroads)

ARTILLERY RIDES THE RAILS

The Civil War brought forth a radical departure in the artillery field when rail-borne guns were used in the art of warfare. The Baldwin Locomotive Works had constructed an armored car equipped with a revolving rifled gun as early as 1861 and this car or others of a similar type were used on lines in the border regions threatened by Confederate raiders.

During the Peninsular Campaign of 1862, the Confederates used a piece of railway artillery with good results. General Robert E. Lee advocated this weapon, writing to his Chief Engineer, Major W. H. Stevens, that he suspected the Yankees were constructing a railroad battery and that he thought a similar battery would prove effective in combatting General McClellan's advance. Lee sent letters to others with the same suggestion, including Col. Josiah Gorgas, Chief of the Confederate Department of Ordnance, Capt. Geo. Minor, Chief of Ordnance & Hydrography of the Confederate States Navy, and to President Jefferson Davis. The result was a rifled and banded 32-pounder, weighing 5,700 pounds, designed by Lt. John Mercer Brooke of the Confederate Navy; another Confederate naval officer, Lt. R. D. Minor, designed the mounting and equipment. This railway battery, commanded by Lt. James E. Barry, was used in the Seven Days Battle around Savage's Station on the Richmond & York River Railroad and proved very effective.

A similar use of a railroad battery by the Confederates was recorded when the Union forces occupied Jacksonville, Florida, in early March of 1863. The Confederate forces under General Joseph Finegan were encamped about 10 miles west of Jacksonville on the line of the Florida, Atlantic & Gulf Central Railroad, and the use of railway artillery was planned by Lt. Thomas E. Buckman, in charge of General Finegan's ordnance. A large 8-inch rifle of English manufacture was mounted on a flat car and placed in charge of Pvt. Francis Sollee, 1st Special Battalion, Florida Volunteers. The Confederates warned the Union commander, Colonel Higginson, to evacuate the women and children prior to the shelling of Jacksonville. Actual firing commenced about 3:30 A.M. on March 25th, 1863, from a distance of about $1\frac{1}{2}$ miles and some seven rounds were fired into the city before the Federal gunboats on the St. Johns River found the proper range and shelled the Rebel battery, forcing the train to withdraw.

After morning guard mount, the Yankees ventured forth to cut the railroad line about 4 miles west of Jacksonville, making it impossible for the Confederates to get within range. With them went a 4-inch rifle, mounted on a small flat car and pushed along the rails by manpower. As they neared their objective point, the Rebels came steaming around a curve with their railroad battery shoved by a woodburning locomotive. A brief artillery duel took place before the Confederates fell back, the first Rebel shell killing one Union soldier marching along a nearby road and wounding several others, one of them fatally.

During the advance on Richmond in 1864, the Union forces used at least two rail batteries, in addition to the big mortar used at Petersburg. A flat car was outfitted in the Atlantic & North Carolina R.R. shops at New Bern, mounting a field piece behind a barrier of oak planking sheathed with iron. The second car, shown here, was similar in design but mounted a naval howitzer.

READY TO RAMBLE

The locomotive UNION of the U.S. Military Railroads is shown in this old photo taken at Alexandria, Virginia. The UNION was built by Baldwin in 1862, bearing Shop No. 1061.

The use of passes was a source of much trouble in the early days of the conflict. Passes were issued indiscriminately by many Army officers, and the privilege of free transportation was so abused that Military Railroad officials had to take drastic steps to remedy the situation. The action taken was very effective, as illustrated by an incident related by General Haupt. Shortly before the battle of Fredericksburg, the Rev. Alexander Reed, General Agent of the Christian Commission, called upon Haupt in an attempt to get a pass over the road to the front, where he was to attend to the distribution of several carloads of hospital supplies. Reverend Reed had applied for a pass to General Halleck, to the Secretary of War, and even to President Lincoln, but had met with a refusal in each instance, since all passes had been prohibited. General Haupt appreciated the urgency of the merciful mission and penned the following message:

"Alexander Reed is hereby appointed brakeman in the service of the Military Railroad Department, and will enter upon his duties forthwith. He is directed to report without delay at Falmouth. He will be furnished transportation by boat and rail, and this order will be recognized as a pass by all guards."

When Haupt handed the clergyman this message, the puzzled man of the cloth asked what it meant, stating he knew nothing of the duties of a railroad brakeman. Haupt informed him that it was the only means by which he could grant him transportation, adding "When you get to Falmouth, if you do not like the service you can resign." The happy Reverend Reed was soon on his way to the desired location. Years after the War, Haupt was introduced to Reverend Reed by the pastor of the First Presbyterian Church in Pittsburg. Haupt remarked that they had met before, but the Rev. Reed could not recall such a meeting.

"Perhaps you are ashamed to acknowledge that you once held the position of brakeman on a Military Railroad," ventured Haupt, and this instantly recalled the foregoing anecdote, much to the amusement of both parties.

OLD SCOUT

The locomotive SCOUT of the United States Military Railroads originally bore the name ECLIPSE. When the Virginia Central Railroad was moving General Lee's army west for the campaign around Cedar Mountain in 1862, a shuttle service was inaugurated between Richmond and Gordonsville, Virginia; trains of about 15 cars each were made up at 17th Street in Richmond, run to Gordonsville, unloaded, and sent back to Richmond for reloading. The crews involved kept this movement up for 10 days and nights without relief, sleeping for brief intervals in their clothes while delayed at various points for short periods of time. Named locomotives and their engineers involved in this exhausting movement included the STAUNTON, Martin R. Alley; ALBEMARLE, John M. Kraft; J. H. TIMBERLAKE, John Horton; WESTWARD HO, John Davidson; E. H. GILL, Geo. W. Pelter; JOHN TIMBERLAKE, Robert Murray; CHAS. ELLETT, John Dunn; GREENBRIAR,

Raymond T. Dunn; MILLBORO, Seth Mack; MONTICELLO, Fendall W. Ragland; JEFF KENNEY, Tunis Swartz; STUART, Wm. Keaton; M. W. BALDWIN, Simon Ailstock; C. G. COLEMAN, L. S. Alley; C. R. MASON, Westley P. Huntley; E. FONTAINE, R. J. Goodwin; and the BEAUREGARD, Engr. James McCandlish. The BEAUREGARD and the JEFF DAVIS were captured on the Alexandria, Loudon & Hampshire Railroad in 1861 and given good Confederates names by the Virginia Central; a third engine captured at the same time became the JOHNSON on the Richmond, Fredericksburg & Potomac lines under Southern control.

The U.S. Military R.R. engine SCOUT, pictured here, has been listed as a New Jersey Locomotive & Machine Company product, but in all probability that identification is erroneous. Evidence indicates she was built by the Jersey City Locomotive Works in Jersey City, New Jersey; this firm succeeded the New York Locomotive Works operated there by Breese, Kneeland & Company.

(Courtesy of Ansco Brady collection)

LINCOLN PASSED THIS WAY

This view of Hanover Junction, Pennsylvania, has been the center of much dispute among historians and scholars. President Lincoln moved through this rail junction on his way to deliver the famed address at Gettysburg, and some contend that he is the tall figure in the top hat standing at the right of the locomotive. The controversy still exists, and no positive proof has been found to settle the question.

During the campaign for Gettysburg, the activities of Herman Haupt and his railroaders played an important role. Using the tracks of the Western Maryland Railroad, Northern Central Railroad, Hanover Branch Railroad, Franklin Railroad, and other lines, supplies were moved to the front and trains loaded with wounded hurried to the rear. Among the wounded evacuated was the dashing General Daniel E. Sickles, who had lost a leg in the Gettysburg battle; Haupt found the wounded officer near Hanover and provided him with transportation to Washington.

To expedite repairs on the lines shattered by Confederate forces in the Gettysburg area, Haupt has his Construction Corps rushed up from Alexandria. The crews brought power, split wood for the engines, track material, and 25 yoke of oxen for transporting repair supplies along the ruined lines.

Haupt had resided in Gettysburg and was thoroughly acquainted with the region. When it became apparent that General Meade was not following up his defeat of Lee's forces, Haupt mounted a locomotive and made a wild night dash to Washington to urge that the Federal troops strike the fleeing Confederates and crush them before they could cross the Potomac. Haupt's advice to Meade, his former West Point class-mate, went unheeded and Lee made good his escape.

Haupt complained of the customary confusion caused by the various departments of the Federal forces after the Gettysburg battle. In a message to General Montgomery C. Meigs, Haupt reported that the roads were blocked with trains of supplies ordered sent to Gettysburg, held there, and finally returned without ever being unloaded, while the wounded lay for hours awaiting transportation tied up in the senseless movements of Quartermaster supplies. Military interference with the smooth operations of his railroads was a constant thorn in Haupt's side and he never ceased to fight for a system which would enable the rail lines to function to the best of their ability.

RAIL SPLITTER?

This enlargement of the figure reputed to be President Lincoln in the Hanover Junction scene fails to establish positive identity, but it does present a good view of the cap-stacked locomotive standing at the station. Note the big boiler check valves, the roofed shelter over the front of the tender, and the signal lanterns displayed beneath the oil headlight bracket; the engineer and fireman gaze at the camera from their respective sides of the cab.

(Courtesy of the National Archives)

WHITE OAK SWAMP

The actual location of this photo by Brady or one of his operators has been the subject of some dispute. Some sources place it at Blackburn's Ford, Virginia, but that locale appears on old maps at some distance from the Orange & Alexandria Railroad. The view was probably taken at White Oak Swamp on the line of the Richmond & York River Railroad about the time of the Seven Days' Battle, when McClellan's forces were retiring toward Malvern Hill. The United States Military Railroad controlled 20 miles of the railroad between White House Landing on the Pamunkey River and Fair Oaks Station and this portion of the line was abandoned after the collapse of the campaign in the region.

The U.S. Military Railroad locomotive SPEEDWELL, acquired second-hand from the Old Colony & Fall River Railroad, was among the engines lost to the victorious Confederates when the Army of the Potomac was forced back to Harrison's Landing in the last days of June, 1862. The engine was used on the Richmond & York River road by the captors and was renamed the CHICKAHOMINY; she was recovered in 1865 and sold to O. H. Donovan for $5,000.

In June of 1864 the Federal forces returned to the Richmond & York River Railroad and operated the line between White House and Despatch, about 14 miles, for a period of about 10 days, after which it was abandoned by order of General Grant and the rail torn up and removed to Alexandria.

Contemporary sources state that some of the old rail from the Confederate-held portions of the Richmond & York River were used in 1863 in construction of the Piedmont Railroad from Danville to Greensboro; the Piedmont was seized by the Federal army and for a short time was held by the Treasury Department as confiscated property of the government of the Confederate States of America. Organized in 1862, the work on the Piedmont Railroad was backed by the Richmond & Danville Railroad and the Confederate States War Department and was directed by Capt. Edmund T. D. Myers, C.S.A. Labor shortages forced the road to purchase slaves, many of whom ran away; rails were in short supply and the 48-mile line was not completed until late in May, 1864.

TRANSPLANTED NEW ENGLANDER

Hinkley & Drury built this 4-4-0 for the Old Colony & Fall River Railroad in 1846 and she was named the JOB TERRY. She bore Shop No. 83, had 15x20 inch cylinders, 54 inch drivers, and weighed 42,000 pounds. The JOB TERRY was purchased by the United States Government on March 18, 1862, and the engine was taken to the U.S. Military Railroad operations in Virginia. Two other Old Colony & Fall River engines also were purchased for Government service. These were the SPEEDWELL, a Lawrence Machine Works 4-4-0, and the SENTINEL, formerly named the DORCHESTER. This engine had been built by Seth Wilmarth in 1849.

Shortly after the JOB TERRY was placed on the Military lines, General John Pope retreated from Manassas toward Fredericksburg and the locomotive was left behind, falling into the hands of the Confederates. After being captured on the Orange & Alexandria, she was apparently sold by the Con-federate Government to the Wilmington & Weldon Railroad in North Carolina. She remained on this line during the war, serving alongside the three new Baldwins purchased by the road in 1859. These Wilmington & Weldon engines were named the GOV. ELLIS, P. K. DICKENSON, and GILBERT POTTER.

In 1872 the JOB TERRY was renumbered Wilmington & Weldon No. 1, and was rebuilt in 1873, having the bell off a Mason engine applied to her. She was renumbered Wilmington & Weldon No. 111, and later became Atlantic Coast Lines' No. 411. She was sold to the Williams & McKeithan Lumber Company in November, 1903, and reportedly was still in service until 1911.

The old JOB TERRY is shown here as Wilmington & Weldon's No. 111, heading Train 59 at Hobgood, North Carolina, in 1890.

(Courtesy of Dr. S. R. Wood)

COL.A.BECKWITH   UNITED STATES MILITARY R.R.D.S

100

GRANT'S HEADQUARTERS

In June of 1864 General U. S. Grant began his campaign to invest Petersburg and capture the Confederate capitol of Richmond by a move from the south. To supply his troops in this maneuver, he ordered the occupation of City Point, Virginia, a landing on the James River at the junction of that stream and the Appomattox. The old City Point Railroad had connected the terminal with Petersburg by a line running west, on the south side of the Appomattox River, but the wharves at City Point had been destroyed earlier in the war.

The Military Railroad set about to rehabilitate the terminal facilities and repair the railroad. Near the end of June the road was in operation to Pitkin Station, about 8 miles west of City Point. Wharves were erected, a roundhouse built, and Army supplies and rolling stock were shipped in; regular train service was started by July 7th, 1864, much of the rail in use being salvaged from the Richmond & York River Railroad.

J. J. Moore was detailed to survey a new rail route around the south side of Petersburg in July and nine miles of this new road, called the City Point & Army Line, was completed by early September. The new road ran from Pitkin Station to Yellow House, the Fifth Army Corps headquarters on the Weldon River, crossing the Norfolk & Petersburg Railroad and the Petersburg Railroad. In November this new road was extended about 2¼ miles to Peebles House over some stiff grades, and in December a branch was constructed from Hancock Station to Fort Blaisdell.

Typical of the motive power used on the City Point road was the COL. A. BECKWITH, shown here near Grant's headquarters at City Point. This engine, formerly named the P. H. WATSON, was built by R. Norris & Son and was received by the Military Railroad on June 23rd, 1863. She was a standard 4-4-0 type, a wood-burner with a screened funnel stack and equipped with a cross-head cold water pump. Note the arched entry into her wooden cab and the port-hole style windows in the rear cab walls. At the close of the war the COL. A. BECKWITH was sold to the Baltimore & Ohio Railroad for $10,500.

In the background of this photograph can be seen the footpath and crude steps cut into the bank, leading up to the buildings and tents that housed General Grant's headquarters.

WATERFRONT SCENE

This view taken at City Point shows an engine of the U.S. Military Railroad switching on the banks of the James River; at left stands a six-horse team hitched to a freight wagon. Horses played an important role in the Civil War as cavalry mounts, artillery teams, and draught animals for the endless wagon trains used to haul military supplies. In regions not served by rail or water transport, the horse or mule was indispensable.

The fill in the foreground nearly conceals the low trestles supporting the yard tracks leading to the wharves; the track work and the big warehouse behind the locomotive was a Construction Corps achievement.

(Courtesy of the National Archives)

(Courtesy of the National Archives)

JAMES RIVER TERMINAL

Focal point for activities on General Grant's City Point & Army Line, operated by the U.S. Military Railroads, was the home terminal at City Point, Virginia. This view shows the enginehouse, water tanks, and three locomotives of the Military Railroads. The engine in the right foreground, with her tender reversed, is the PRESIDENT, an old Eastwick & Harrison 4-4-0 confiscated by the Federal forces from the Winchester & Potomac Railroad which ran out of Harpers Ferry.

The cars coupled ahead of the PRESIDENT are loaded with material being used to create a fill to the left of the three tracks leading into the enginehouse; a track was later laid on this fill leading to a turntable, which was installed at the left of the enginehouse.

Water supply for both men and locomotives often created a serious problem. The water at City Point was of very poor quality and typhoid was prevalent there. On the longer runs in Tennessee, special crews were detailed to water service; construction engines got their water from wells, springs, or streams via a bucket brigade of Construction Corps employees using buckets or even camp kettles. Customarily, water tanks were erected near a suitable supply in advance of regular train service. E. C. Smeed has stated that no fixed rules were followed in constructing the water tanks, but that they were generally wooden tubs about twelve feet in diameter and eight feet deep, placed upon a framed stand.

The new trackage constructed for the City Point & Army Line had a number of short, steep grades and an officer who viewed the passage of a train over this road likened its progress to that of a fly crawling over a washboard.

A distinguished passenger on the Military Railroad out of City Point was President Abraham Lincoln. Accompanied by his wife and son, the Chief Executive arrived there aboard the steamboat, RIVER QUEEN, about 9:00 P.M. on the night of March 23rd, 1865. The following morning he boarded a train and rode up toward the front, where bitter fighting was still going on. Lincoln conferred with Generals Grant, Sherman, and Admiral Porter, and remained in the vicinity until Petersburg was captured on April 2nd. The Confederates evacuated Richmond on April 3rd and shortly thereafter Lincoln visited the fallen capitol of the Confederacy. The surrender of General Lee at Appomattox on April 9th spelled the end of a long and bitter struggle.

MILITARY MERRY-GO-ROUND

The turntable erected by the Construction Corps alongside the enginehouse at City Point is depicted here; the wooden walkway circling the outer circumference of the table provided footing for the crew who pushed the turntable around with manual effort while engaged in turning a locomotive. The covered vehicle in the left foreground may have served as a travelling studio for the Army photographer engaged in preserving the scenes of war-time railroading for posterity.

(Courtesy of the National Archives)

B-3426

RAILROAD CAMP

This view at City Point, Virginia, shows the camp facilities located on the railroad at Grant's headquarters on the James River. Note the wigwam-shaped Sibley tents and the bower covered with branches, the latter to provide shade and shelter from the scorching summer sun.

In the background at left is the U.S. Military Railroad engine, GENL. DIX, a 4-4-0 built by Baldwin in December, 1862. She bore Shop No. 1095, had 16x24 inch cylinders, 60 inch drivers, and was named in honor of General John A. Dix. The woodburner at right is reportedly the GENL. McCLELLAN, another U.S.M.R.R. locomotive built by New Jersey Locomotive & Machine Co. in 1862, along with the COL. McCALLUM, RED BIRD, and GOVERNMENT.

Unsanitary conditions, contaminated water, and exposure caused sickness to decimate the ranks of soldiers and civilian railroaders during the Civil War. Accidents also took their toll of the civilian employees of the Military Railroad and the Construction Corps. The Army would not furnish medical care for these hired civilians, so the employees formed the U.S. Military Railroad Hospital and donated 1% of their wages to hire a contract surgeon. In the Department of the Mississippi this hospital association was in charge of Dr. R. I. Furgharson, with Mr. John Trenbath serving as treasurer.

The Military Railroad Hospital served the men well, and the only complaint arose on one occasion when the funds supplied by the employees' donations ran low.

When the War ended, the hospital organization was disbanded, leaving quite a fund of surplus cash in its treasury. The employees presented this fund to W. W. Wright, the Chief Engineer, as a token of their esteem. Colonel McFerran, Assistant Quartermaster in the Department, learned of this fund and demanded that it be turned over to the Quartermaster Department as Government funds, but General McCallum, the General Manager of the Military Railroads, advised Wright to keep it as being rightfully his. McCallum cited the fact that it had accumulated from voluntary donations made by civilian employees, and clinched his argument with the opinion that had a deficit existed in the employees' hospital fund, no power on earth could have moved the Quartermaster Corps to pay up the bills.

DISASTER AREA

This view shows a part of the wharves and rail yards at City Point after the disastrous explosion of August, 1864. A barge loaded with munitions exploded, killing a number of men employed in the area and causing the destruction shown here. Note the vast amounts of military stores piled on the wharves between the railroad tracks and the James River. Armies travel on their stomachs and the Military Railroad transported huge quantities of rations for the troops and forage for their animals.

(Courtesy of Ansco Brady collection)

(Courtesy of Norfolk & Western Railway)

THE PETERSBURG EXPRESS

When the Union forces laid siege to Petersburg, Virginia, in 1864, a heavy sea-coast mortar was used to bombard the city. Called the "Dictator" by the Federal troops, this mortar was mounted on a platform car and moved along the tracks to various locations for firing, a method calculated to prevent Confederate artillery from finding its range. The train assigned to handle this railroad battery was nicknamed "The Petersburg Express."

The huge mortar, cast by Mr. Chas. Knapp in his Pittsburg iron works, weighed 17,000 pounds and had a 13 inch bore extending 35.1 inches from muzzle to base. The projectiles fired by the "Dictator" were 200 pound exploding shells, normally sent on their way by a 20 pound charge of powder, although a 75 pound charge was rated as the maximum. In actual use, 14 pounds of powder proved sufficient for the approximate range of two miles, and this charge caused the mortar to shift nearly two feet on the car; the car itself was forced backward about twelve feet by the recoil. The mortar crew was directed by Colonel H. L. Abbott of the First Connecticut Heavy Artillery. The huge weapon was brought to City Point by ship and mounted on the car which ran on a branch of the South Side Railroad.

The terrific force of the explosions of the mortar's shells wrought havoc in the Confederate lines and silenced a number of their batteries on Chesterfield Heights. One round blasted a Confederate field-piece and its carriage over the parapet which had been protecting it, but the defending troops soon learned to dodge the ponderous balls, their burning fuses tracing their flight at night. For a time the "Dictator" was mounted in a semi-permanent location at the end of a spur track in a ravine near the Jordan House.

PETERSBURG YARDS

Located on the Appomattox River, Petersburg, Virginia, was a vital Confederate railroad junction point. The Richmond & Petersburg Railroad ran north to Richmond, the Norfolk & Petersburg Railroad extended southeast to Norfolk, the South Side Railroad ran west to Lynchburg and a direct line of connections to Tennessee, Alabama, and the Mississippi, and the Petersburg Railroad ran south to connect with lines spreading a network through North Carolina, South Carolina, and Georgia. In addition, the little City Point Railroad's line ran from Petersburg to City Point landing on the James River. This view taken after the fall of the city shows the remains of burned cars at the far left and the cupola-topped station at right.

ARMY LINE STATIONS

The upper photograph shows Union troops guarding supplies at Cedar Level Station, Virginia, in December of 1864. The lower photo shows a spur near Yellow House, with Army wagon trains loading supplies from the freight cars spotted behind the earthworks in the distance. Both of these stations were located on the City Point & Army Line operated by the United States Military Railroads. The rail line supplied vast quantities of rations and equipment to the Federal soldiers besieging Petersburg, while the gallant defenders under General Lee were at the point of starvation.

(Virginia Historical Society photos, courtesy of National Archives)

TEEMING TERMINUS

City Point mushroomed into a lively port when Grant established his base of supplies here. This view, with Bermuda Hundred in the distance, shows the depot buildings and wharves of the Military Railroad while construction was still progressing. The broad bosom of the James is dotted with vessels of every type, including steam propellers, tugs, big sidewheelers with walking beam engines, barges, and a variety of sailing vessels. In addition to being a vital supply depot, City Point was also the locale of the exchange of prisoners of war. Note the brush bower shading the mess tables in the foreground, with the table service in place for a meal for the hungry railroaders.

MILITARY STOREHOUSE

The board and batten building in this scene was one of the Commissary warehouses located at City Point, Virginia. Behind the horse-drawn freight wagon at right stands one of the Norris locomotives used on the City Point & Army Line Railroad built by the Construction Corps to supply Grant's troops. The combination of Virginia rains and the hooves and wheels of Army supply wagon trains created the seas of mud visible in the foreground. Wagon roads were turned into quagmires and the sticky mud slowed marching troops and bogged their artillery and commissary wagons, but the use of railroads for transport surmounted these obstacles.

Not only did the railroads provide improved transport for troops, guns, and supplies, but they also furnished locomotives for the swift movement of dispatches and special trains to carry Army officers rapidly from one location to another.

When General Ambrose Burnside was commanding the Union forces during the Fredericksburg campaign, the U.S. Military Railroad kept a locomotive under steam at Falmouth, on the Richmond, Fredericksburg & Potomac Railroad, ready to handle a special train whenever General Burnside ordered it. On one occasion during the month of January, 1863, the General ordered his train made ready at 9:30 P.M., but failed to appear at the designated hour, a common-place occurrence. Meanwhile, a derailment blocked the road at Stoneman's Sta-

tion and Supt. W. W. Wright ordered the General's locomotive to the scene to assist in clearing the line. Before the wreck was cleaned up, Burnside arrived at the Falmouth depot at 11:10 P.M. and became quite impatient when he found that his special was not available. He started walking down the track toward the scene of the derailment and had gone some distance when he met the engine returning to Falmouth. Unfortunately, the engineer failed to recognize the pedestrian officer in the inky darkness and passd him up. When the light engine reached Falmouth, the mistake was discovered and the locomotive hurriedly ran back until the irate Burnside was found, picked up, and carried to the terminal at Aquia Creek. The angry Burnside stormed into the office of Supt. Wright and demanded to know who was responsible for the night's actions. Wright handed him Haupt's instructions relating to the superiority of train movements; after reading them, Burnside wheeled out of the office with the remark: "This is a nice condition of things if the General in command of an army can be snubbed by a brigadier!"

Haupt was informed and supported Wright in his actions, at the same time urging him to conform with General Burnside's orders, stating that Wright would be held blameless for any delays which might occur if Burnside demanded the regular trains side-tracked to permit the movement of his special.

SOUTH SIDE RAILROAD DEPOT

The South Side Railroad Company was chartered in March, 1846, and construction of this line through the Old Dominion State began in October, 1849. The main line of the South Side extended for 123 miles from Petersburg to Lynchburg, Virginia, and was completed in November, 1854. The City Point Branch, 10 miles long, was built under the charter of the Appomattox Railroad, a concern that was sold in foreclosure to the City of Petersburg; the City Point line was purchased from the City of Petersburg by the South Side Railroad and played a vital role in the Union Army advance on Petersburg.

At Lynchburg, the South Side connected with the Virginia & Tennessee Railroad, a concern chartered in 1849; the V&T was the direct connection linking Virginia with Tennes-see and the border states to the west. The V&T began construction in January, 1850, and was completed in the spring of 1857, extending 204 miles from Lynchburg to Bristol, where a connection was made with the East Tennessee & Virginia Railroad to carry the cars on to Knoxville, Chattanooga, and western points. The Virginia & Tennessee, the South Side, and the 81-mile Norfolk & Petersburg Railroad were organized into the Atlantic, Mississippi & Ohio Railroad in 1870, under the guidance of President William Mahone, a former Confederate General known as the "Hero of the Crater."

This 1865 view shows the Petersburg station of the South Side Railroad in use by the Quarter Master's Department while the Union Army was occupying Petersburg; note the covered wagon used to haul supplies.

(Courtesy of the National Archives)

RUINS OF RICHMOND

This badly battered locomotive of antique design was photographed in the remains of the Confederate Capitol in 1865; the city had been one of Virginia's most important railroad centers, and was the home of the noted Tredegar Iron Works, one of the major locomotive builders in the South. Conductor Carter S. Anderson, who ran trains on the old Virginia Central Railroad under the Confederate flag, left a highly interesting account of a war-time incident in Richmond. Shortly before the Seven Days' Fight and the battle of Malvern Hill, the Yankees under General McClellan were threatening to overrun the city and Supt. Whitcomb and Pres. Fontaine of the Virginia Central were seeking a way to evacuate their priceless engines and rolling stock; although a number of Southern roads entered Richmond, the Central had no physical connection with a route over which the equipment could be moved to safety. A temporary track was laid on the surface of the street up Broad Street Hill from the Virginia Central tracks at 17th Street to the Richmond, Fredericksburg & Potomac depot at the corner of 8th and Broad Streets; the grade was very steep, about 350 to 375 feet to the mile. Engineer Fendal Ragland and his engine, the old MILLBORO, were chosen to make the first climb; Yardmaster Dandridge Lowry had a force of men with chocks on hand to block the locomotive if it should stall. The first attempt was a failure, the MILLBORO slipping down on the steepest part of the grade at Jail Alley. Ragland backed her down the hill and Supt. Whitcomb suggested he let some of the other men try, but Ragland argued for a second chance, which was granted. After oiling the old gal, Ragland gave her an affectionate pat and said: "Well, old girl, you and me will be in Hell or at the Powhatan Hotel (the top of the hill) in ten minutes!" The engineer then pulled his throttle wide open and the locomotive bounced and roared up the hill to the cheers of the large crowd gathered on the scene. As Ragland drew to a triumphant halt at the Powhatan Hotel, he was greeted by Mr. Scammel, the proprietor, who informed him that one of the servants had just "found" a bottle of rye whiskey in the lumber room and that Scammel wanted Ragland to help him "hide" it. Richmond was under a strict Confederate prohibition law at the time, but Scammel operated a boot-leg setup; the proscribed bottles were passed from a storeroom into the hotel's lumber room through some loose bricks and into the waiting hands of the "finder."

After Ragland had proven that engines could negotiate the temporary track up the steep grade, other Virginia Central locomotives made the ascent successfully.

COSTLY DEBRIS

The gaunt stone piers in this photo mark the remains of the lengthy Richmond & Petersburg Railroad bridge across the James River at Richmond, Virginia. The piles of cannon balls and rubble in the lower right foreground mark the ruins of the great Confederate arsenal, destroyed by fire when Jefferson Davis and his staff evacuated the city in the face of the Union advance.

SCOURGED BY FLAME

These three views graphically illustrate the devastation wrought upon the railroad equipment during the evacuation of Richmond, Virginia, in 1865. President Jefferson Davis was attending St. Paul's Church on Sunday, April 2nd, when he received a message from General R. E. Lee that Petersburg was about to fall and that the Richmond capital must be abandoned. A train soon rumbled out of town, bearing Davis and members of his government, and the night that followed was one of holocaust. Public buildings and the big arsenal were fired, with resulting explosions spreading the fires over the city. Railroad bridges, depots, and shop facilities were left a mass of charred wood and crumbled masonry. Scenes such as these greeted the Union troops entering the fallen stronghold of the Confederacy. Note the odd side rods on the inside-connected 4-4-0 in the upper photo. Below is a view of the trucks of burned cars, and on the opposite page is a general view of the grim destruction, reportedly showing the Richmond & Petersburg terminal with the scorched remains of what may be a Denmead 4-4-0 standing desolately in the ruins.

(Upper and lower photos, Library of Congress; opposite page, Virginia Historical Society photo, courtesy of National Archives)

HIGH BRIDGE

The great wooden truss bridge of the South Side Railroad over the Appomattox River in Virginia was known as the "High Bridge" and was reportedly the second highest span on the North American continent at the time of the Civil War. The wooden portion rested on more than 20 brick piers and was 128 feet above the water; the entire bridge was about 2,400 feet long. The broad stretch of bottom land in the foreground was under water when the Appomattox was at flood stage. Some concept of the size of this structure can be had by comparing it with the figure of the man standing near the base of the first pier at left.

Upon the evacuation of Petersburg, the Confederates fired this bridge on the morning of April 7th, 1865. The pursuing Federal forces managed to extinguish the blaze after it had destroyed about four spans, shown here at left. The firefighters accomplished their task while skirmishers were still popping away in the immediate vicinity. The temporary trestle work shown in this photo by the noted Alexander Gardner carried the trains safely across the Appomattox at slow speeds until permanent repairs were made.

SOUTH SIDE TRESTLE

This wooden trestle was located on the South Side Railroad near Petersburg, Virginia. The road ran west from Petersburg to Lynchburg, crossing the Richmond & Danville Railroad at Burkeville. The Confederates under General Gordon attempted to destroy the South Side line in their retreat from Petersburg. In the foreground can be seen the cut stone ruins of Lee's Dam.

(Courtesy of the National Archives)

THE WOOD BUTCHERS

This scene depicts the lumber yards of the Construction Corps located along the Potomac River in Alexandria, Virginia. The workmen are carpenters, engaged in dressing planks for use in construction work; note the tholepins set into the timbers to hold the planking in a vertical position to enable the men to smooth the edges with hand planes. In the right background, a locomotive of the U.S. Military Railroad stands coupled to a platform car.

A wide variety of experimental work was carried on by the Construction Corps under Herman Haupt at the Alexandria terminal. Here was perfected the design for arks, a rather crude but capable type of boat used for many purposes. These craft were 60 feet long, 20 feet wide, and from 6 to 8 feet high; the main portion of them consisted of poles hewed flat where they rested on each other, then a vertical siding of two-inch planks, a double thickness of pitched canvas, and a final outer covering of boards.

When lashed together in groups of four, they formed a rough car float 120 by 40 feet, capable of carrying 16 freight cars; the weight of a standard locomotive depressed an ark only 8 inches, making them suitable for use as pontoons to support rail lines across wide and deep streams.

(Courtesy of the National Archives)

117

CAROLINA INTERLUDE

A woodburner of the U.S. Military Railroads poses for her photo on the trestle over Little River during the operations in North Carolina; coupled behind the locomotive is a primitive caboose lettered "Conductor's Car No. 1" and bearing the initials of the Atlantic & North Carolina Railroad. A water tank stands at the far end of the bridge over the stream, which furnished the water supply for the locomotives. Note the stacked muskets with fixed bayonets in the foreground, evidence that the War was probably still in progress.

The U.S. Military Railroad began operations in North Carolina in February, 1865, when a force of men landed at Morehead City. The 95 miles of track of the Atlantic & North Carolina R.R. was repaired and opened for service from Morehead City to Goldsboro by March 25th, 1865. In addition, the Military Railroads took over the North Carolina R.R., Goldsboro to Charlotte, 223 miles; the Wilmington & Weldon R.R., 162 miles; and 25 miles of the Raleigh & Gaston R.R. from Raleigh to Cedar Creek. General McCallum's report states that 38 locomotives were used by the Military Railroad in North Carolina, along with 422 cars; 3,387 men were employed on the lines, laying or relaying 30 miles of track and erecting 3,263 lineal feet of bridges.

The retreating Confederates had destroyed much of the A&NC track around Kingston and Batchelor's Creek and large numbers of Negro laborers were hired to replace the line under Foreman E. C. Smeed. Crews worked both day and night, and a shortage of ties developed; soldiers were then detailed to serve as tie-cutters and they turned out 5,400 rough-hewn ties in two days to replenish the supply.

Before the advent of the Military Railroads on the North Carolina scene, the 44 miles of the Atlantic & North Carolina Railroad lying between Morehead City and Batchelor's Creek was being used by Federal forces, and was operated under the control of the depot quartermaster stationed in New Bern.

In the face of the Federal invasion, most of the rolling stock and locomotives had been evacuated from the Atlantic & North Carolina ,being taken inland to Salisbury via the North Carolina Railroad and thence up the Western North Carolina R.R. line extending from Salisbury to a point west of States-

ville. The Military Railroad sought out and returned most of the missing A&NC equipment, with the exception of the locomotive HAWKS, which was trapped beyond a burned-out bridge. They also recovered the engines captured from the North which had been used in North Carolina.

(Courtesy of the Library of Congress)

GRIM REMINDER

War is hell and this locomotive bears mute testimony to the destruction the conflict between North and South left in its wake. The old 4-4-0 shown here has been scourged by fire, losing her wooden cab and pilot; the naked brick shells of the gutted buildings in the background have suffered the same fate. The exact location of this scene is not recorded, but was probably in the ruined Confederate capitol city of Richmond, Virginia.

(Courtesy of Thomas Norrell)

CEDAR CREEK TRESTLE

This view shows the wooden trestle erected by the U.S. Military Railroads over Cedar Creek, on the Raleigh & Gaston Railroad in North Carolina during the closing days of the War. The conductor's car coupled behind the 4-4-0 is probably in use as a travelling studio for the photographer who recorded the scene. The original bridge at this site was destroyed during the War and the replacement span pictured here was built by members of the Construction Corps. The structure was reportedly 530 feet long and 88 feet high, and was erected in 72 hours.

Railroad bridges in North Carolina suffered the fate that befell so many similar facilities throughout the War of Secession. When the Federal invaders hit Weldon, North Carolina, they found a fine wooden railroad span with masonry piers crossing the Roanoke River; this bridge was used jointly by the Petersburg Railroad, the Seaboard & Roanoke Railroad, and the Wilmington & Weldon Railroad. The Yankees placed four or five locomotives of the Wilmington & Weldon road upon the bridge, along with all the freight cars it would hold, and fired the structure. The flames destroyed the bridge and cars, allowing the locomotives to fall into the river; the last one was not fished out of its watery resting place until 1868.

The Civil War also brought about a number of novel uses for locomotives. During the Federal operations on the James River, a locomotive was loaded aboard a flatboat and used to furnish power for a piledriver. At Port Hudson, Louisiana, the Confederates used an engine to power a grist mill manufacturing corn meal for their forces; this engine probably belonged to the little Clinton & Port Hudson Railroad. Contemporary sources state that the locomotives used on Federal hospital trains had their stacks and jackets painted a brilliant shade of scarlet and that three red lanterns hung beneath their headlights served to identify them at night. The Rebels apparently respected these trains of mercy and afforded them a measure of immunity. One of Confederate General Nathan Bedford Forrest's scouts is reputed to have flagged a Yankee hospital train and directed the crew to head into a side track when Forrest's raiders were engaged in tearing up the tracks and destroying other trains in the area.

(Courtesy of the Library of Congress)

(Courtesy of the National Archives)

EQUIPMENT LANDING

This view, reportedly taken at Manchester, Virginia, shows rolling stock being landed at a wharf for the United States Military Railroads. A number of box cars can be seen on the Schuylkill barges lying at the dock, while numerous car wheels line the track at the right. Such a display of rail equipment must have seemed like a dream to the metal-starved railroad men of the Confederacy, whose rolling stock had dwindled alarmingly from lack of material for repairs.

Even after the hostilities ended, the flow of railroad equipment into the South continued. About 24 new locomotives, ordered from various Northern builders for use on the U.S. Military Railroads, arrived at City Point, Virginia, on June 1st, 1865. The Army no longer needed this motive power and it was shipped on up to Manchester for storage. The Federal Government later auctioned off the engines and cars, most of them going to the battered rail lines within the former

Confederacy. A contemporary report of 1866 mentioned the sale of one locomotive and eleven cars from the surplus stored at Manchester to the Alabama & Florida Railroad. Other surplus equipment was being offered for sale in the North in September of 1865, including six locomotives at the Portland Locomotive Works in Maine, four locomotives at the Hinkley Works in Boston, fifty box cars in Pennsylvania, and eighty-four box cars at Wilmington, Delaware.

During the early years of the War, supplies were rushed to the Military Railroad service in lavish quantities, but after rumors of speculation and fraud began to haunt the Army, an elaborate system of red tape was inaugurated. Harried railroad storekeepers were confronted with a mountain of paper work consisting of reports, forms, and requisitions. One of the major headaches was the completing of inventories; under actual operating conditions, new stores of wood for locomotive fuel was piled on top of the wood on hand, new supplies of tallow and oil dumped into barrels partly filled with old lubricants, and spikes, waste, and other items being delivered were unceremoniously mixed with the stock held in store. To attempt to render an accurate inventory of stores received and stores on hand proved to be well-nigh impossible. However, a system was established, storehouses provided, and requisitions drawn for small tools and supplies, thus giving the Government a better check on expenditures and tons of reports and forms covering items ranging from track spikes to locomotives.

THE NUT-SPLITTERS

This view from the C. B. Chaney collection of photographs in the Smithsonian Institution is reported to show the locomotive HOMER of the United States Military Railroads, a Mason-built eightwheeler. The engine was probably one of a number delivered to the Government after the shooting war had ended; orders had been placed for locomotives prior to the final surrender of the Confederate forces, and many of these engines were delivered to Manchester, Virginia, where they were stored and later sold. The mechanical force pictured here may be engaged in assembling one of these engines after delivery from the Mason factory.

(Courtesy of Smithsonian Institution)

WAR'S AFTERMATH

This photo at an unidentified location shows a group of U.S. Military Railroad men with sets of car wheels and piles of metal debris gathered from along the war-torn rail lines serving the Civil War battlefields.

(Courtesy of National Archives)

123

MILITARY MOTIVE POWER

Shown in the upper view on this page are three locomotives of the U.S. Military Railroads at City Point, Virginia, water tanks. Engine in the foreground is the GENL. J. C. ROBINSON, a Mason product formerly named the GENL. HAUPT. Locomotive at left rear is probably the LT. GENL. GRANT, while the obscured engine at right rear is thought to be the GOVERNOR NYE.

The dim, faded engine in the lower view is the E. J. M. HALE of the U.S.M.R.R., built by Amoskeag Manufacturing Co., Manchester, New Hampshire, in 1856, Shop No. 203, for the Manchester & Lawrence R.R., whose equipment was pooled with the Concord Railroad. Three other engines from this pooled power were acquired by the U.S.M.R.R.; these were the THORNTON, renamed SENATOR; ROB ROY, renamed A. A. BUNTING; and the EPPING. The BUNTING and a second-hand New Jersey Loco. & Machine Works engine bearing the number, 2, were lost at sea in a wreck while bound for New Bern, North Carolina. The E. J. M. HALE was renamed the COL. WEBSTER and in 1865 was sold to the North Carolina Railroad, who renamed her the NAT BOYDEN. The photo shown here was reportedly taken while in service on the Military Railroad lines in North Carolina.

(Upper view, courtesy of Library of Congress; lower view, courtesy of Thomas Norrell)

POSTWAR MOTIVE POWER

Southern railroads suffered a great deal of damage during the Civil War, and the peace after Appomattox saw most of the lines sadly lacking in engines fit for service. The Wilmington & Weldon Railroad purchased two new locomotives from William Mason's works in February, 1866, to help carry on the job of reconstruction in the battered South.

The EDWARD KIDDER, shown here, was built under Mason's Shop No. 225, and had 14x22 inch cylinders and 60 inch drivers. The second Wilmington & Weldon Railroad engine built at the same time was Mason's No. 226, and had the same specifications; this second locomotive was named the S. L. FREEMONT. These engines were assigned road numbers 33 and 34, later renumbered 95 and 96 under the Atlantic Coast Line operating association control, and later became Atlantic Coast Line's 401 and 402; the 401, the former EDWARD KIDDER, was sold on March 18, 1901, to an unknown buyer.

The Wilmington & Weldon Railroad was one of the South's pioneer rail lines. It was chartered as the Wilmington & Raleigh Rail Road Company in 1833 and was opened for traffic on March 7, 1840. On February 14th, 1855, the name was changed to the Wilmington & Weldon Railroad. The main line consisted of 161.25 miles of standard gauge track connecting Wilmington and Weldon, North Carolina. At Weldon, the Petersburg Railroad formed a connection north to Petersburg, Virginia, and the Raleigh & Gaston Railroad formed a western link to Greensboro and the western portion of the state. An important junction point on the Wilmington & Weldon was located at Goldsboro, North Carolina. Here the Atlantic & North Carolina Railroad ran easterly to the port at Morehead City, and the North Carolina Railroad ran west and south to Greensboro, Salisbury, and Charlotte, North Carolina. The latter road, 223 miles long, was chartered in 1849, started construction in July of 1851, and was completed on January 30th, 1856.

The Construction Corps of the U.S. Military Railroads opened the Wilmington & Weldon road for Federal use in April, 1865, forming an auxiliary supply line to Sherman's army; the main artery of this supply route was the Atlantic & North Carolina Railroad line from Morehead City to Goldsboro.

(Courtesy of Atlantic Coast Line Railroad)

WESTERN WAR EFFORT

Motive power and rolling stock of the Illinois Central, pictured here, moved Union troops and supplies in support of the North's war efforts. Railroad men not only served on the home front, but many flocked to the colors and joined fighting outfits. Locomotive engineer George Bentley raised a volunteer company of railroaders in the Chicago area and marched away to war; killed in action, Bentley was but one of many to give his life for the Union. His sword was returned to Supt. Geo. L. Dunlap of the Chicago & North Western, who had been a great admirer of the plucky engineer.

In August, 1862, a "Railroad Regiment," the 89th Illinois Volunteer Infantry, was recruited from railroads around Chicago. This group was commanded by Col. Charles T. Hotchkiss of the Galena & Chicago Union Railroad. The "Railroad Regiment," some 900 strong, moved out of Camp E. H. Williams on September 4th, 1862, and were in action in Kentucky shortly after. The unit fought valorously at Murfreesboro (Stone River), through the Tullahoma campaign, and such major engagements as Chickamauga, Missionary Ridge, Resaca, the march on Atlanta, New Hope Church, Kenesaw Mountain, and the battles against Hood's forces at Columbia, Franklin, and Nashville, Tennessee. At Missionary Ridge "C" Company, composed of men from the Chicago & Milwaukee Railroad, lost their captain, former locomotive engineer Henry L. Rowell. Engineer George Sinclair, another former runner, was shot through the left lung at Liberty Gap, but the ball passed entirely through his body and he lived to run his engine for many years after the conflict ended.

During the War, the 89th had been recruited up to 1,400 men; over 700 of these brave lads were lost in the bloody battles participated in by the "Railroad Regiment," and the unit lost one Lieutenant Colonel, seven Captains, and four Lieutenants.

Illinois Central's engine No. 152 was built by Rogers Works at Paterson, N.J., in 1856. Engine 31, with a gaily-painted tender, was rebuilt to a coal burner by the Illinois Central in their Chicago shops. Engine 83, sporting two steam domes, is a typical wood burner of the Civil War period.

(Courtesy of the Illinois Central Railroad)

CUMBERLAND POWER

The Memphis, Clarksville & Louisville Railroad formed a strategic link in the chain of rail lines connecting Kentucky with the city of Memphis.

The locomotive C. A. HENRY, pictured here, was built by Baldwin for the Memphis, Clarksville & Louisville in 1860, under Shop N. 964, and is fairly representative of the motive power on the road at the outbreak of the War.

To hold the region along the western Kentucky-Tennessee border, Confederate General Albert Sidney Johnston was forced to spread his troops in a thin line. The Mobile & Ohio Railroad terminus at Columbus, Kentucky, was held by the figfhting bishop, Leonidas Polk, and a force of about 10,000; some 4,000 more Confederates were located around Bowling Green on the Louisville & Nashville under the command of Simon Bolivar Buckner, while additional troops under Felix K. Zollicoffer controlled the Cumberland Gap region.

Bowling Green, Kentucky, became the headquarters for a Rebel force numbering about 20,000 troops under the command of General William J. Hardee. Under this command, a loose military control was set up, embracing the Louisville & Nashville and the Memphis road. A civilian superintendent, G. B. Fleece, was placed in charge of this phase of Confederate transportation.

When the Union forces drove the enemy south, the standard gauge Louisville & Frankfort and the Louisville & Lexington roads were broadened to 5-foot gauge by the Federals at a cost of $27,914.56. The Memphis, Clarksville & Louisville and the connecting Edgefield & Kentucky were used in the summer of 1864 to move military trains from the Cumberland River to the huge Army supply depots established in Nashville.

(Baldwin Loco. Works negative, courtesy of H. L. Broadbelt)

TENNESSEE TRESTLE WORK

This view shows the timber trestle located on Section 49 of the Nashville & North Western Railroad, between Nashville and Johnsonville. The Norris-built locomotive at right is probably the engine assigned to carry Photographer J. F. Coonley over the lines operated by the U.S. Military Railroads.

The wooded hill country of Tennessee provided ideal cover for Confederates and guerrilla raiding parties bent on burning railroad bridges and wrecking trains. A contemporary account by a Confederate engaged in these attacks behind the Union lines indicates that the raiders were equipped with a portable metal device which could be placed inconspicuously upon the rail to throw a locomotive into the ditch, and gives an account of a derailment caused by this contrivance on the high fill on Kenesaw Mountain, Georgia.

The success of these raids upon the Union-held rail lines is cited in a report rendered by General D. C. McCallum. He states that in the last six months of the fiscal year ending June 30th, 1865, the Military Railroad wrecking train picked up and carried into Nashville 16 wrecked locomotives and 294 carloads of car wheels, bridge irons, and other railroad material salvaged from wrecks caused by guerrillas and rebel raids.

Not all damage to railroad equipment was caused by enemy action, however. In one instance the locomotive of a U.S. Military hospital train ran low on water while ascending a steep grade. The brakemen tied down the hand brakes on the cars and the engine was uncoupled and proceeded up the mountain, running for water at a tank located several miles ahead.

128

While ascending the hill toward the tank, the light engine met a train bound down the mountain. The engineer of the hospital train engine, believing a head-on collision inevitable, reversed his locomotive and jumped off. His engine stopped before it hit the opposing train, then took off in reverse, running wild down the grade. The speeding locomotive crashed into its own standing train, crushing the flimsy wooden cars and killing many of the wounded troopers aboard.

George Herrick, Superintendent of the Car Department at Nashville, built a wrecking car which was used for picking up locomotives and cars following the accidents that occurred on the Army-controlled lines.

SURFACING TRACK

This 1863 view shows a track gang at work on the Nashville & Chattanooga Railroad near Murfreesboro, Tennessee, shortly after the Battle of Stone's River. Note the light rail spiked to hewn ties without benefit of tie plates, and the dirt ballast being worked by the gandy dancers. Lack of crushed rock or gravel ballast caused the earthen roadbeds to become extremely rough when churned into mud by heavy traffic in the rainy seasons; the worst of the soft spots in the track were frequently raised by the use of wooden slabs or wedges inserted under the sunken portions.

(Courtesy of Library of Congress)

(Courtesy of Library of Congress)

FORTIFIED PORTALS

This railroad bridge over the Cumberland River at Nashville, Tennessee, was equipped with watchtowers and heavy timbered doors for protection against enemy action. The doors and the heavy timbered sheathing on the sides of the wooden truss were pierced with embrasures to afford the defenders a wider range of fire in case of a raid or attack.

The first railroad bridge across the Cumberland into Nashville was put in service in October, 1859, and tested with three locomotives; the structure was built jointly by the Louisville & Nashville Railroad and the Edgefield & Kentucky Railroad. This photograph was probably taken by Geo. N. Barnard in 1864.

129

CIVIL WAR RAILROAD PRESIDENT

Shortly before the actual start of the Civil War, the internal affairs of the Louisville & Nashville Railroad erupted in a battle between the directors of that line, and the president, Kentucky-born pro-slavery John M. Helm, was replaced by James Guthrie, whose likeness appears here. Guthrie was also a native of the Blue Grass State and a man of wealth and position. He had served as Secretary of the United States Treasury while President Franklin Pierce was in office, and he took charge of the Louisville & Nashville line on October 2nd, 1860. Guthrie continued to hold the office of president of the L & N until June 11, 1868.

When the opening shot burst over Fort Sumter in the Charleston harbor, Guthrie's railroad consisted of some 269 miles of track, a stud of some 30 locomotives, and about 300 freight and passenger cars, all built to 5 foot gauge; when the Louisville & Nashville was chartered to build south from Louisville, Kentucky, in 1850, a gauge of 6 feet was selected, and some track and motive power of this width was acquired, but was discarded in favor of the 5 foot gauge. The main line into Nashville, Tennessee, was completed in November, 1859.

The position of the road was both enviable and dubious. The heavy flow of traffic into Dixie taxed the capacity of the line's equipment as the South attempted to stock up on vital supplies, and even after the actual shooting started, contraband shipments moved North in large quantities. On the other hand, the line ran through a border region and was subjected to devastating raids, and guerrilla bands frequently plundered the heavily-laden trains.

Although loyal to the Union cause, Guthrie's first concern was his duty to his railroad and its investors, a situation that was to lead to later problems. He quarreled with William P. Innes, the superintendent of railroad transport under General Rosecrans; Innes and Charles A. Dana accused Guthrie of giving preference to commercial shipments instead of the less lucrative Government traffic, and Guthrie in turn charged that the contracts between his road and the Government were being violated. Some of this difficulty may be traced to Guthrie's relations with John B. Anderson, a Louisville & Nashville transportation department man who was placed in charge of railways under Government control in the Departments of the Ohio, the Tennessee, and the Cumberland in 1863 and removed under a cloud in 1864.

IMPRESSED SWITCHER

When the Civil War broke out, the Nashville & North Western Railroad, chartered in 1854, had about 25 miles of road in operation from Nashville to Kingston Springs, Tennessee; in addition, some grading had been done on the westward extension toward the Tennessee River. In February of 1864, General Grant placed the road under the control of General D. C. McCallum and construction work was pushed, bringing the railhead to a terminus on the Tennessee River named Johnsonville. This new construction, giving the road about 78 miles of track, was completed on May 10th, 1864, and operations turned over to the U.S. Military Railroads on the 9th of August, 1864. Although exposed to frequent guerrilla raids and considerably damaged by them, the road was a vital link in the Union supply route when the Cumberland River was at low water. Traffic was heavy throughout August, September, and October of 1864, but on November 4th the Confederate General Forrest planted his batteries on the west bank of the Tennessee and practically demolished the extensive warehouses, docks, and terminal facilities at Johnsonville, causing the Yankees to pull out. On the 30th of November all rolling stock and equipment was moved back to Nashville and the road was abandoned; when Confederates of Hood's command occupied the country in early December, they destroyed all of the bridges on the line. These were replaced by Union

(Courtesy of R. B. Carneal)

forces in January of 1865, and many of them were again lost to the floods that swept the region later that spring, some of them being rebuilt three times. Permanent truss bridges replaced the spans in May and June of 1865 and the road was returned to its owners on September 1st of that year.

Engine No. 3, shown here, was an 0-4-0 saddletank with the old hook valve motion built for the Nashville & North Western by Rogers in August, 1860 and was one of the locomotives captured by the U.S. Military Railroads and used by them during their operations in Tennessee, retaining her original number on the U.S.M.R.R. roster.

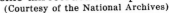

STATE ROAD CAR SHED

This substantial structure served the Western & Atlantic Railroad in the Chattanooga, Tennessee, terminal; it stood near the passenger station and was located near the Crutchfield House, a prominent Chattanooga hostelry. A similar Western & Atlantic car shed in Atlanta was blown up by Sherman's men before they evacuated the city. The terminal facilities of the W&A in Chattanooga were extensively remodeled in 1881, and the present Union Station there has a part of the car shed shown here incorporated into the rear of it; the old GENERAL is housed in a part of this original shed.

The locomotive popping off in the arched entrance to the shed has lost her stave pilot in some unrecorded mishap.

(Courtesy of the National Archives)

TENNESSEE TERMINAL

The important railroad center of Nashville played a vital role in the military operations of the Civil War. Here the southern terminus of the Louisville & Nashville Railroad was located, connecting with the Nashville & Chattanooga Railroad leading into the heart of the Southern Confederacy. The short Nashville & North Western also entered the city, and the larger Tennessee & Alabama Railroad ran south to a connection into Decatur, Alabama; at Edgefield Junction, north of Nashville, the Edgefield & Kentucky road joined the main line of the Louisville & Nashville.

Lack of motive power hampered the Military Railroad operations out of Nashville during the increased activities of the Army in 1863, forcing Secretary of War Edwin Stanton to confiscate three locomotives being built by Baldwin for the old New York & Harlem rail line presided over by Cornelius Vanderbilt. Appeals were sent by Stanton to other locomotive builders early in 1864, and soon a number of new engines were arriving in Nashville for military service.

A large locomotive repair shop and machine shops placed in service at Nashville employed about 3,000 men, while the extensive blacksmith shops, containing 40 forges, was staffed by a force numbering nearly 200; the monthly pay-roll and operating expenses amounted to around $2,000,000. By 1865 the Construction Corps had provided facilities for over 90 engines in repair shops or storage at Nashville, in addition to having erected their own barracks and mess facilities and having aided in erecting fortifications around the city when it was threatened with an attack by Confederate General John B. Hood.

This view of the Nashville engine facilities was taken from Church Street, looking north, and shows at least 20 locomotives. The engine at far left, standing in front of the entrance to the roundhouse, is U.S. Military R.R. No. 131, while No. 132 stands in the immediate foreground; both of these were built by Danforth, Cooke & Co. in 1864.

Scaffold work in the distance beyond the enginehouse roof marks the erection of a large stack, probably for the stationary engine used in the shops.

The low-numbered box cars in the left foreground are probably in service as cabooses or "conductor's cars"; note the application of windows and side steps and ladders leading to the side doors. The wooden boxes with circular holes cut in them, mounted at opposite ends of the cars, could hold a lantern to serve as a crude marker on the rear of the train for night operations.

(Courtesy of National Archives)

HOME FROM THE WAR

When the Confederate forces under General Johnston were forced south after the surrender of Fort Donelson in February of 1862, the Union troops commanded by General U. S. Grant occupied the key city of Nashville, Tennessee. Rebel stores and equipment was hastily evacuated, quantities of it moving over the Nashville & Chattanooga and the Tennessee & Alabama railroads. The Louisville & Nashville Railroad, just

completed in 1859, lost considerable rolling stock during the Union advance, the cars and engines being carried off to Dixie by the retreating Confederates. Included in the loot were five nealy-new 4-4-0 type locomotives, all built by Moore & Richardson in 1859-60. These included Engines 20, 23, 24, 27, and 29; No. 20, named the QUIGLEY, is shown here at Louisville, after her return to the L & N in 1865. She was rebuilt in 1870 and was scrapped in 1885. All five of the Moore & Richardson engines confiscated by the Confederates in 1861-62 were returned in 1865-66; Engine 24 had been sold by the Confederate Government to the 5 foot gauge Charlotte & South Carolina Railroad, running between Charlotte, North Carolina, and Columbia, South Carolina, via Chester, before her recovery by the Louisville & Nashville management.

The trackage and equipment of the L & N suffered considerable damage during the course of the war in the west. Engine No. 6, the MARION, was blown up during the war; she was a 4-4-0 built by Moore & Richardson in their Cincinnati Locomotive Works in Ohio in 1857, and in 1869 was rebuilt as a 2-6-0 type.

(Courtesy of Louisville & Nashville Railroad)

133

MOTIVE POWER FOR THE WEST

Rogers Locomotive & Machine Works turned out the funnel-stacked American type shown here for the United States Military Railroads, where she bore No. 116. The locomotive was intended for use on the lines operated by the Government in the Department of Tennessee and the Mississippi, and was built to a gauge of 5 feet. The early operations of the railroads serving the Union armies in the Western Theater were under control of the Quartermaster Department and the situation there became so chaotic that in the spring of 1863 Secretary of War E. M. Stanton directed General Herman Haupt to inspect the western lines and render a report on their conditions. Haupt, busy with preparations for Hooker's coming campaign, sent Mr. F. H. Forbes, a Massachusetts newspaper reporter, to carry out the desired inspection. Forbes, a personal friend of Gen. Haupt, made a lengthy investigation and rendered a report that created some consternation, since it pointed out that waste, inefficiency, and speculation were hampering the railroads in the area.

Pressure was brought to bear upon Haupt to suppress the Forbes report, but the doughty Pennsylvanian refused to do so and sent the report to Stanton, along with numerous suggestions of his own for cleaning up the mess. Quartermaster General Montgomery Meigs went West to inspect the supply lines and in December of 1863 General D. C. McCallum was directed to move a part of the Construction Corps into Tennessee to inspect the rail lines and aid in making necessary repairs. McCallum prepared a report pointing out the deficiencies of the existing railroad operations in the region and in February of 1864 General Grant relieved John B. Anderson and appointed McCallum as General Manager of Military Railways in the West.

(Courtesy of R. E. Prince)

CONFEDERATE DRAFTEE

M. W. Baldwin & Co. built four locomotives in 1860 which were delivered to the Louisville & Nashville Railroad early in 1861. These locomotives bore Shop Nos. 982, 983, 986, and 988, and introduced a new feature in engine construction; a modification of the Baldwin 4-6-0 type, the locomotives were fitted out with the Bissell pony truck and radius bar, and were of the 2-6-0 wheel arrangement. They had 18 inch cylinders, 52 inch drivers, and weighed 65,000 pounds. Louisville & Nashville assigned them road numbers 35, 36, 37, and 38. When the Confederate forces withdrew from Nashville they carried Engine 38 into Dixie with them and she was used on various lines in the South until the end of the rebellion.

When the shooting was over, the thrifty Northerners who controlled the Louisville & Nashville sent agents into the South and most of the "borrowed" motive power was traced down and returned to the company. Engine 38, shown here, was brought back to the L & N in 1868; in 1872 she was rebuilt, emerging as a conventional 4-6-0 type. After another rebuilding in 1878, the old war veteran was scrapped in 1891.

In 1862 the Baldwin Works turned out some more engines of the 2-6-0 wheel arrangement, built with 18½ inch cylinders; these engines went to the Louisville & Nashville and to the Dom Pedro II Railway of Brazil. The engines of this type for the Brazilian line were the first Baldwins to be fitted with steel tires, and these tires had to be imported from abroad; Baldwin kept a stock of 500 of these imported tires on hand for use as replacements.

(Courtesy of National Archives)

MARCH OF PROGRESS

M. W. Baldwin constructed this 4-4-0 in his Philadelphia works in May, 1864, for the United States Military Railroads of Tennessee and Mississippi. The engine bore Baldwin Construction No. 1240, and was assigned U.S.M.R.R. road number 156. Note the two boiler check valves on this locomotive; the forward boiler check was a part of the cold water crosshead pump, while the check valve behind it was connected to the delivery pipe of a steam injector. The body and piping of this injector can be seen between the two driving wheels.

The injector was the invention of a prominent French engineer, Henri Jacques Gillard, and was first patented by him on May 8th, 1859. In that year the device was introduced in England by Sharp, Stewart & Co., and the American patent rights were acquired by William Sellers & Company of Philadelphia. This firm began to manufacture injectors in 1860 and their use gradually spread. The Academy of Science in Paris awarded Gillard the grand mechanical prize for his invention in 1859, but engineers in America were slow to accept them, being adverse to change from the familiar old crosshead pump to the unknown injector. The Rogers Locomotive & Machine Works applied the injector to some of their engines in 1861. The invention made it possible to put water into the boiler when the locomotive was not in motion; with the old style of pump, which took its power from the movement of the crosshead, the locomotive had to be moving in order to operate the pump.

136

RUNNING WATER BRIDGE

This large timber trestle was located on the Nashville & Chattanooga Railroad in Tennessee, a vital link in the supply route for Sherman's forces during the Atlanta campaign. The road was subjected to frequent raids and lost many of its bridges, some of them destroyed and rebuilt four or five times during the course of the War. The Military Railroad replaced much of the line's old U-shaped rails with T-rail while in charge of the road, and extended sidings to accommodate the heavy military traffic. About 130 miles of the Nashville & Chattanooga's 151-mile main line was reconstructed and 45 water tanks erected to supply the locomotives.

Rail traffic on the road kept the operating crews extremely busy as supplies were rushed to Chattanooga for Sherman's army, and as many as 160 of the 10-ton freight cars in use poured into the busy terminal in a day. The cost of labor and railway material expended on the road by the Government in 1864-65 amounted to more than $4,000,000.

Not all traffic was bound for the front, however, and the trains returning from Chattanooga carried increasing numbers of sick and wounded Union soldiers, discharged veterans, refugees, captured Confederates, freed Negro slaves, and quantities of material the Army saw fit to send to the rear.

Much of the credit for opening the line into Chattanooga must go to E. C. Smeed, who supervised reconstruction of the damaged bridges. General McCallum and Supt. W. W. Wright were in New York recruiting railway men when Smeed arrived on the Nashville & Chattanooga, but both arrived back at the front in time to ride the first train over the rebuilt road into Chattanooga.

(Courtesy of National Archives)

STEAM IN NASHVILLE

This photo depicting some of the United States Military Railroads' motive power was taken near Church Street in Nashville, Tennessee, with the State Capitol building dominating the hill in the right background.

The city was the southern terminus of the Louisville & Nashville Railroad, a line that suffered greatly from the ravages of war. One of the first blows fell on the L&N in late 1861 when Confederate General Simon Bolivar Buckner seized the main line between the Tennessee state line and Lebanon Junction, along with the Memphis branch. Forced to retreat by the troops of the Home Guard under General Sherman, Buckner's forces carried off engines and rolling stock and destroyed the Green River bridge, one of the largest on the road. When Federal troops under General D. C. Buell captured Nashville in February of 1862, they found that the rebels had practically destroyed the L&N from Bowling Green on south.

The long bore at South Tunnel, Tennessee, had been sabotaged when the Confederates rolled freight cars into the tunnel and fired them. The blaze spread to the tunnel's timbering and when the fire died out, shale and dirt had blocked the bore for about 800 feet.

The raiding cavalrymen under Confederate General John H. Morgan hit the L&N time and again, burning depots, bridges, and wood yards. Gallatin, Tennessee, suffered from Morgan's raids, and at a point near Cave City, Kentucky, the raiders applied the torch to an L&N freight train, leaving 37 cars a smouldering ruin of ashes and warped iron. Later the big Salt River bridge at Shepherdsville was destroyed by rebel forces, water pumping stations along the road were laid waste, and the track forces driven off. Section hands were left without food or housing and the wood for the locomotives had to be hauled long distances to replace the stores burned by the Confederates.

General Morgan's Christmas raid into Kentucky in 1862 left about 35 miles of the L&N in smoking ruins, and shortly after the Federal forces had restored operations on the road, heavy rains deluged the region and swept away practically all of the small bridges on the line.

NASHVILLE HEADQUARTERS

This view, taken near the Church Street depot of the Nashville & Chattanooga Railroad in Nashville, contains a number of interesting details. The large wooden frame two-story building in the center is being completed by Union forces to house the offices of the United States Quartermaster and the Superintendent of the United States Military Railroads.

The box car in the left foreground bears the lettering of the Adams Express Company. By arrangement with the Military Railroads, private express cars were moved in and out of the war zones in limited numbers; they brought coveted packages from home to the men at the front, containing the little luxuries soldiers yearned for. The cars returning from the front carried sadder cargo, often being piled with coffins containing the bodies of men killed in battle and being returned to their homes for burial by relatives who had searched the battlefields to locate the remains of their loved ones.

At the lower right can be seen the front end of one of the odd self-propelled steam coaches used by the U.S. Military Railroads; plainly visible are the headlight, bell, whistle, cylinder, and a portion of the driving gear of this unusual piece of equipment. Military records concerning these steam-driven coaches do not seem to exist, but a contemporary source stated that in 1863 the War Department requisitioned three "steam cars" from the Pittsburgh, Fort Wayne & Chicago Railway.

. (Courtesy of the National Archives)

PHOTOGRAPHER'S SPECIAL

(Courtesy of the National Archives)

A highly interesting branch of U.S. Military Railroad service in Tennessee was the photographic train, operated to aid in securing a pictorial record of the transportation achievements of the Federal forces. J. F. Coonley, a photographer, was instructed by the Quartermaster Department to take pictures of all bridges, trestles, buildings, boats, and railroad facilities used by the Department. He was provided with a locomotive and a box car fitted out as a travelling studio and sent out to cover the operations in the Department of the Tennessee. Coonley covered the railroads from Louisville, Kentucky, to Atlanta, Georgia, including all the lines out of Nashville, the road south to Decatur, Alabama, the Huntsville area, and the East Tennessee & Georgia Railroad from Chattanooga to Knoxville.

Coonley's photographic car is probably the piece of rolling

stock coupled behind Engine 56 in this photograph showing bridge No. 2 over Sullivan's Branch on the Nashville & North Western R.R. The car contained darkroom and living facilities, including a stove, cooking gear, bunks for five men, and a barrel of water, the latter serving both the domestic and photographic needs of the outfit. In his reminiscences, a member of this entourage recalls that the staple items of the bill of fare aboard the photographic train were tough mule meat and boiled potatoes.

Coonley and his party were officially acknowledged to be operating in a "super-hazardous location" and an armed guard of soldiers was detailed to protect the unit. Rebel forces made several attempts to capture the photographic train, but the crew beat hasty retreats and managed to elude them.

RAPID TRANSIT

After the defeat of the Union forces under General Rosecrans at Chickamauga in the fall of 1863, it was decided to move General Hooker's 11th and 12th Corps from Virginia to Alabama to reinforce the Federal troops there. Civilian railroad officials and military officers planned the transfer and the first troop trains rolled over the Orange & Alexandria R.R. and into Washington on September 25, 1863, in cars borrowed from the Baltimore & Ohio. The movement over the Orange & Alexandria was directed by General D. C. McCallum, while the operations from Washington, D.C., to Jeffersonville, Indiana, were supervised by John W. Garrett, president of the Baltimore & Ohio, and W. P. Smith, B & O Master of Transportation. South of the Ohio River, Thomas Scott, John B. Anderson, Frank Thomson, and Montgomery Meigs directed the troop trains to their final destination near Bridgeport, Alabama. By 10:00 A.M. of September 25th, three trains totaling more than 60 cars had carried about 2,000 troops through Martinsburg, the sections running 30 minutes apart; behind these advance units, 9 more trains bearing 7,000 men had passed Relay House. When the first troop train was steaming into Benwood on the morning of September 27th, a total of 12,600 men, 21 cars of baggage, and 33 cars of artillery had passed west from Washington. A pontoon bridge was thrown across the Ohio between Benwood and Bellaire for the transfer of the troops, and after minor delays at Indianapolis, the trains arrived at Jeffersonville and the troops were ferried across to Louisville and sent out on the Louisville & Nashville Railroad. The first four trains chuffed up to the ruins of the destroyed span at Bridgeport, Alabama, on September 30th; by October 8th, the last of the 23,000 men had arrived.

In two weeks, this major movement had shifted the huge previous military transport records. This Civil War era view of the Baltimore & Ohio shops at Martinsburg, West Virginia, shows some of the typical motive power in use at the time of this troop movement.

(Courtesy of Thomas Norrell)

PRISONERS OF WAR

These photographs show a group of captured Confederates at Chattanooga, awaiting shipment by rail to a Northern prison camp. Yankee writers have constantly harped on the horrors of such Confederate prisons as Andersonville and Libby, but they fail to mention the fact that over 26,000 Confederates died while being held in the dank prison camps of the North.

Not all of the Confederates who were captured on the field of battle were delivered to Yankee prisons. The author's great-grandfather, Samuel Creson, was a member of a volunteer cavalry company composed mainly of Kentuckians. He and a number of his comrades were captured and loaded aboard a prison train, but plotted to escape if possible. Armed guards were stationed on top of the box cars comprising the train, while other armed guards were stationed at the open car doors. The men watched carefully and the moment came when conditions favored their plan of escape. The old woodburning engine was battling a steep grade, the track running along the top of a high, sandy fill with a dense cover of brush and timber at the bottom; at a pre-arranged signal, the daring prisoners grabbed the door guard and toppled him backward into the car, then dove from the train and rolled down the steep embankment. The guards on the car tops loosed a ragged volley of musket fire but their aim was poor and the little group of escapees gained the safety of the sheltering woods as the train rattled on up the mountain.

MILITARY BLOCKHOUSE

The novel wooden structure shown here was erected for the defense of the U.S. Military Railroad yards at Chattanooga, Tennessee. This view, looking toward Fort Jones, shows a formation of Union infantry detailed to garrison the loop-holed log fort; in the center background can be seen a part of the railroad roundhouse, and the stack of a locomotive appears over the building at the extreme right.

Photographs of the numbered 5-foot gauge locomotives of the U.S. Military Railroads showing this blockhouse in the background have appeared in other publications, with the location erroneously given as Front Royal, Virginia, etc.

The neatly-tended walk and garden in this photo bear

mute testimony to the fact that guard duties at this point were not very strenuous, provided ample time for the men to be detailed for sprucing up the grounds in order to keep them busy. The life of the guards who garrisoned the blockhouses strung along the rail lines through the Cumberland Mountains was equally dull, although occasionally spiced with action when attacks were made by Confederate raiding parties. The loneliness of the men stationed at these isolated outposts was graphically depicted by the pathetic little signs they erected along the track, "Please Throw Us A Paper."

Although soldiers were used as guards and occasionally as laborers employed in cutting ties and aiding the Construction Corps, their services were not always satisfactory. General Haupt reported that General Burnside had ordered 200 soldiers to assist in reconstruction of the bridge across the Rappahannock at Fredericksburg, but that when the battle started these men drifted away, scattering over the hills and behind trees. The civilians employed by the Construction Corps were still at their post when Haupt arrived, even though enemy shells had cut the ropes of the block and tackle used for hoisting bridge timbers; Haupt ordered the men to a position of safety and the work was resumed the next day, but abandoned when the Union forces were driven back from Marye's Heights.

On another occasion, troops were ordered to remove the planking from the deck of a railroad bridge where it had served as a walkway. The work was carried out at night, and the soldiers removed some of the rails along with the decking and gave no warning of this action to the operating railroaders. A train attempted to cross the bridge and the locomotive jumped the gap safely, but the tender and 7 cars were derailed and severely damaged, 3 of the cars being destroyed.

The wooden frontier-type blockhouses offered protection against rifle fire but could not resist concentrated shelling by artillery. In the fall of 1863, the Confederates sent an Irish ex-bartender, Dick Dowling, with about 50 men, to spike the guns of Fort Griffin to prevent them from falling into the hands of a Yankee fleet. Upon arrival, Dowling decided to make an attempt to hold the fort, which guarded the Sabine Pass on the Gulf Coast of Texas. He and his men barricaded the fort with rails removed from the Eastern Texas Railroad, withstood a bombardment, and by a ruse captured two of the Union gunboats.

LOOKOUT MOUNTAIN

The towering peak overlooking Chattanooga and the Tennessee River was the site of the famous Battle Above the Clouds, where Union and Confederate forces were locked in deadly combat in late November of 1863. The Union forces led by General Peter J. Osterhaus struggled up the rough, rocky slopes in the face of blazing muskets, fighting their way through a dense afternoon fog that blanketed the heights. The Confederates withdrew from their beleaguered position in the night and the Union forces followed up their advance on the next day, soundly whipping Confederate General Braxton Bragg's troops in the Battle of Missionary Ridge.

This view by Army photographer R. M. Cressey, made under the direction of Capt. Wm. E. Merrill, shows the tracks of the Nashville & Chattanooga Railroad as they passed under the rocky flank of Lookout Mountain; the roadbed was located on a narrow shelf at the foot of the mountain and followed along the banks of the Tennessee River.

(Courtesy of the National Archives)

MOUNTAIN OUTPOST

This Civil War view shows the high wooden trestle on the Nashville & Chattanooga Railroad at Whiteside, Tennessee, located at the pass in the Raccoon Range west of Chattanooga. In the foreground can be seen the tents and a log blockhouse of the United States troops assigned to guard this vulnerable timber structure. The struggles between Union and Confederate forces in the West increasingly centered around the major rail lines as the War progressed and the vital importance of rail transport became indelibly impressed upon the leaders of both North and South.

When the Construction Corps opened the Nashville & Chattanooga Railroad after the battle of Corinth to supply General Buell's advance toward Chattanooga, the thin ribbon of rails was a target too valuable to be overlooked by the Confederates. Rebel troopers led by General Nathan Bedford Forrest spurred their mounts along the track, overpowering the small garrisons stationed in their primitive blockhouses, and cut the line in numerous places. The smoke of burning bridges and trestles curled in the Tennessee skies and the weary forces of the Construction Corps moved into the wake of the raiders to rebuild the burned structures and put the railroad back in operating condition.

When General William T. Sherman made his famous march on Atlanta, Georgia, in 1864, the Construction Corps was ordered to repair the Western & Atlantic Railroad from Chattanooga south in order to supply Sherman's army. One of the major jobs of this assignment was the repair of the burned bridge over the Oostenaula River near Resaca, Georgia. Conservative estimates set the length of time for this task at a minimum of four days, but Sherman reportedly ordered Chief Engineer W. W. Wright to replace the span in 48 hours or take a position in the front ranks. The remains of the former bridge still smouldered as Wright threw a force of 2,000 men into action. Working constantly, the men had the new bridge completed in 72 hours, and Wright reported that the impossible task would have been finished sooner but that the iron-work in the ruins of the old bridge had been too hot to handle when his men began the task of clearing the debris from the site!

(Courtesy of the National Archives)

MESS HOUSES

The United States Military Railroads in the West operated repair shops in Nashville, Knoxville, Chattanooga, and Memphis, Tennessee, and at Huntsville, Alabama; in addition, car repair facilities were located in these terminals, as well as in Atlanta, Georgia, and Little Rock, Arkansas. The mess houses in Chattanooga, shown here, are typical of the buildings erected to feed the Military Railroad employees.

Construction Corps crews were fed mainly on salt beef called "junk" by the men, with rations of hard bread, crackers, coffee, and sugar; an additional half ration was frequently issued if the men were forced to work at night. It is highly probable that the men supplemented this fare by the time-honored Army arts of "scrounging" and foraging.

STATE ROAD DEPOT

This imposing brick structure is the Chattanooga depot of the Western & Atlantic Railroad, owned by the State of Georgia. A short distance to the right of this station stands the "car shed," and nearby is the famous old Crutchfield House, a noted Civil War era hotel. The architecture of this depot and car shed was duplicated in the State Road's Atlanta station buildings; the facilities were mainly built of brick and stone for lasting usage.

(Courtesy of the National Archives)

SEVERED SPANS

This photograph shows the ruins of the Nashville & Chattanooga Railroad's bridge across the Tennessee River at Bridgeport, Alabama, after it was destroyed by the Confederates; it was rebuilt by the Construction Corps in 1863 and used by the United States Military Railroads.

The wooden bridges and trestles of Tennessee and Kentucky offered tempting targets to Confederate raiding parties. One of the best known of Rebel raiders was General John Hunt Morgan, a Mexican War veteran noted for his daring thrusts into Yankee territory. On December 22, 1862, Morgan left Alexandria, Tenn., with about 3,900 men and 7 light artillery pieces, headed for a raid on the Louisville & Nashville Railroad, the vital supply route for Federal General Rosecrans' army. Morgan's raiders were mostly young men, expert horsemen and well mounted; they were poorly armed, some having only shotguns for weapons. The raiders travelled light, carrying 3 days' cooked rations. one blanket, a slicker or overcoat, 2 horseshoes, 12 nails, and their ammunition. Moving over isolated back roads in hilly country, the party covered 90 miles in 3 days, reaching Glasgow, Kentucky, on the evening of Dec. 24th.

After a brush or two with surprised Federal troops, during which they captured Christmas turkeys and supplies, they hit the L&N at Upton's Station on Dec. 26th. From the depot at Upton's, "Lightning" Ellsworth, Morgan's telegraph operator, cut into the wire and sent messages to the startled Yankees in Louisville! The raiders moved swiftly, capturing the Federal block houses at Bacon Creek and Nolin and burning the railroad bridges at those locations. They moved through Elizabethtown on Dec. 27th and on the following day they captured 2 block houses at Muldraugh's Hill, bagging 700 prisoners and a large supply of new Enfield rifles. They burned the two Louisville & Nashville trestles at Muldraugh's Hill, each about 75 feet high and 900 feet long. A detachment of 500 of Morgan's men hit the stockade at Rolling Fork River but were driven off by a relief party of about 3,000 Union troops.

The raiders moved through Bardstown, Kentucky, then on to Springfield and Lebanon, riding through a bitterly cold sleet storm; on December 31st, after 36 hours in the saddle, they arrived in Campbellsville, later moving on to Columbia and Burkesville. On January 2nd, 1863, the weary riders recrossed the Cumberland River and retired behind the Confederate lines, leaving about 60 miles of the Louisville & Nashville in smoking ruins; the road was tied up from Bacon Creek to Shepherdsville until Union forces could repair the damages inflicted by the daring raiders.

---•---

TERMINAL FACILITIES

The three views on this page show the installations used by the United States Military Railroads in Chattanooga, Tennessee. The city was a key point on the rail lines used to carry supplies to General Sherman's troops in their advance to Atlanta. The 288 miles of railway from Nashville to Atlanta was under constant threat of raids by the Rebels, yet it supplied 100,000 men and 35,000 animals during the 196 days of the campaign.

The wear and tear on engines and cars provided plenty of work for the shop forces at the various rail terminals.

Top: The Chattanooga Car Repair Shops.
Center: The Chattanooga Foundry & Car Shops.
Bottom: The Chattanooga Locomotive Blacksmith Shops.
(All three photos, courtesy of the National Archives)

COMMISSARY DEPOT

This Civil War scene shows a locomotive and cars of the United States Military Railroad at the waterfront along the Tennessee River at Chattanooga. This point served as a landing for the steamboats plying the stream in the service of the Federal forces. The Tennessee curves around Moccasin Bend under the ramparts of Lookout Mountain southwest of Chattanooga and the Nashville & Chattanooga Railroad followed the south bank of the stream after crossing Chattanooga Creek. Not far downstream was located "The Suck," a narrow channel where the current was so swift that steamboats had to "line up" over the rapids, winching themselves upstream by means of a line carried ahead and made fast to the bank above the narrow gorge. Before rail connections were restored, Union forces in Tennessee were on short rations and the riverboat route of supply was known as the "Cracker Line." When the trains of General McCallum's rail lines began rolling, an abundant amount of rations and equipment was soon available.

The wooden building behind the locomotive and box cars in this photograph housed the Commissary Department's supplies, while the brick structure at left served as a magazine for powder and ammunition for the guns of the Union armies.

In the background can be seen a part of the wooden wagon road bridge built by Federal troops, linking Chattanooga with the north shore of the Tennessee River.

Northeast from Chattanooga to Knoxville ran the East Tennessee & Georgia Railroad, the only direct link between Virginia and the Confederate forces in the western states. Union forces under General Ambrose E. Burnside occupied the line in the spring of 1864 and portions of it served the Union, although the rolling stock had mostly been evacuated south by the retreating Confederates.

The 112 miles of track connecting Chattanooga with Knoxville was opened up for service by McCallum's Military Railroad personnel in May of 1864. The line was used steadily to supply the Federal troops in the Knoxville area. Also used by the military forces was a portion of the East Tennessee & Virginia Railroad, a line extending from Knoxville to Bristol and a connection with the Virginia & Tennessee Railroad. General Burnside appointed J. B. Hoxie as superintendent of the road, but after it was turned over to the U.S. Military Railroad it was controlled by Superintendent Tallmadge. The line was opened from Knoxville to Bull's Gap in 1864.

ARMY RAILROADERS

Members of the United States Military Railroads' operating and maintenance personnel are grouped around Engine No. 133, an eightwheeler built by Danforth, Cooke & Co. in 1864.

The men who ran the trains for the Military Railroad merited the highest praise for their bravery and devotion to duty. General D. C. McCallum left the following tribute to them in his final report to Secretary of War E. M. Stanton:

"The difference between civil and military railroad service is marked and decided. Not only were the men continually exposed to great danger from the regular forces of the enemy, guerrillas, scouting parties, etc., but, owing to the circumstances under which military railroads must be constructed and operated, what are considered the ordinary risks upon civil railroads are vastly increased on military lines.

"The hardships, exposure, and perils to which trainmen especially were subjected during the movements incident to an active campaign were much greater than that endured by any other class of civil employees of the Government—equalled only by that of a soldier while engaged in a raid into the enemy's country. It was by no means unusual for men to be out with their trains from five to ten days, without sleep, except what could be snatched upon their engines and cars while the same were standing to be loaded or unloaded, with but scanty food, or perhaps no food at all, for days together, while continually occupied in a manner to keep every faculty strained to its utmost."

(Courtesy of Association of American Railroads)

MASTER MECHANIC'S OFFICE

This wooden frame structure, topped with a fancy cupola, was built in Chattanooga to house the Master Mechanic's office of the United States Military Railroads. Because of its strategic location, Chattanooga became an important terminal of Military Railroad operations, especially during Sherman's march on Atlanta. The Nashville & Chattanooga Railroad, 151 miles long, provided the main source of supplies into Chattanooga and also supplied the railroaders with plenty of headaches. General D. C. McCallum. in his report on railroad conditions in the West, has left us this description of the Nashville & Chattanooga's state of disrepair:

"The track was laid originally on an unballasted mud-road bed in a very imperfect manner, with a light U-rail on wooden stringers, which were badly decayed and caused almost daily accidents by spreading apart and letting the engines and cars drop between them."

The Construction Corps was put to work renovating the track, which had deteriorated to such an extent that train speeds averaged only about 8 miles per hour. Mechanical forces set up shop at Nashville and Chattanooga to service and repair the locomotives, and these facilities were equipped with all of the tools and machinery necessary. Confederate railroaders, lacking the Northern resources, had to frequently rely on their own ingenuity. When the C. R. MASON, a tank engine on the Virginia Central, had a driving tire work loose after hard service moving Jackson's troops. her crew improvised a crude forge at Beaver Dam station, using an old iron kettle to hold the charcoal. The tire was tightened up with hand-forged shims and the locomotive was able to proceed to Charlottesville, where she and other Virginia Central engines were ordered to a temporary shop set up at Shadwell for badly-needed repairs.

The C. R. MASON was intended for use as a helper on the steep grade at Millboro tunnel, and her water tank capacity was so small that she was not suited for road service, but a captured Baltimore & Ohio tender was coupled behind her to permit her use on longer runs and the old girl did yeoman duty on the Central's main stem.

(Courtesy of the National Archives)

WESTERN WAR HORSE

Engine No. 162 of the U.S. Military Railroads is shown here, backed by blue-coated Union infantry with fixed bayonets on their muskets; the print was made from a cracked glass plate, with a piece missing at lower left. The 162 was built by Baldwin in 1864, one of a number ordered for service in the Western theater of the War.

One division of the Construction Corps, numbering 285 men, was sent from Virginia to Tennessee in December of 1863 to aid in restoring damaged rail lines; these men were in charge of W. W. Wright, and by January of 1864 they had opened the road from Bridgeport to Chattanooga, finishing the project 3 weeks ahead of schedule. On February 10th, 1864, Genl. McCallum appointed Wright as Chief Engineer of Construction in the Western theater.

To speed up construction of the extension of the Nashville & North Western Railroad, Wright brought 2,000 laborers and mechanics from the North; these civilians were aided by the 1st Missouri Engineer Regiment, the 1st Michigan Engineers, and the 12th and 13th Regiments, Colored Infantry. Wright took charge of the Nashville & North Western and in less than 3 months his forces had finished the extension from Kingston Springs to Johnsonville, turning the road over to the transportation department on June 21st, 1864.

VOLUNTEER STATE VIEWS

The three photographs reproduced here show Civil War railroad operations in Tennessee. At the lower right is a view of the Nashville yards of the Nashville & Chattanooga Railroad. The main line at the right leads to the roundhouse and station buildings visible in the background; note the sets of three-way stub switches. At upper left is a view of the truss bridge over Chattanooga Creek, with Construction Corps members at work on the uncompleted span. This bridge crossed the small creek in the Moccasin Bend district under the northern flank of Lookout Mountain, on the line between Chattanooga and Bridgeport, Alabama. At lower left appears a Tennessee bridge on the Louisville & Nashville Railroad. Early Federal operations of the railroads in Tennessee were marked with turmoil and confusion; under General Rosecrans' administration, his staff issued a flow of orders and counter-orders that snarled train operations, causing Special Investigator F. H. Forbes to advise that complete control of the lines be vested in officials of the U.S. Military Railroad, men who were familiar with rail operations and competent to keep the roads open.

(All three photos, courtesy of the National Archives)

RAILS ACROSS THE RIVERS

The numerous railroad bridges destroyed in the campaigns in Tennessee gave the Construction Corps ample opportunity to ply the skills perfected in Virginia earlier in the War. In the fall of 1863 General Grant had removed John B. Anderson as General Manager of Government Railroads in the Departments of the Cumberland, the Tennessee, and the Ohio. General Grenville M. Dodge was given the task of repairing the Nashville-Decatur line and in 40 days his troops had restored over 100 miles of track, including 182 bridges. Dodge, who was a civil engineer before the War, had rebuilt the ruined Mobile & Ohio in 1862. He later gained wide fame for his work in constructing the Union Pacific.

Upper right: Hiwassee Bridge, on the East Tennessee & Georgia R.R., rebuilt by Construction Corps led by E. C. Smeed.

Lower right: Big Harper Bridge No. 5, Nashville & North Western R.R.

Upper left: Duck River Bridge, Tennessee & Alabama R.R.
(All three photos, courtesy of the National Archives)

MILITARY RAIL SUPPLY

This photo shows the rolling mill built by the Union forces in Chattanooga, Tennessee, to turn out rails for use on the lines of the United States Military Railroads. Old Glory is waving in the breeze and a locomotive of the Military Railroad sends a curl of woodsmoke skyward as the employees pose for the photographer's glass plate exposure.

The tall brick smokestack at the right end of the rolling mill was long a Chattanooga landmark.

STATE ROAD ROUNDHOUSE

This photograph shows the Atlanta roundhouse of the Western & Atlantic Railroad as it appeared in 1864, the year the plate was exposed by Photographer George N. Barnard, under the supervision of Captain (later General) Orlando M. Poe, Corps of Engineers, United States Army. The Western & Atlantic Railroad was constructed by the State of Georgia and the southern terminus was called Marthasville, the name being changed to Atlanta in 1844. Construction began in 1837 and the road was completed into Chattanooga, Tennessee, in 1850.

When the War broke out, the Western & Atlantic was operating a fleet of 46 locomotives, including a new one built in their own shops in 1859-60. The locomotives were wood-burners and the fuel came from the timbered hills along the extremely crooked route of the State Road. In the fiscal year of 1861, the road used over 14,000 cords of wood which cost over $26,000. The freight engine averaged about 30 miles per cord on the Western & Atlantic, while passenger engines such as the SWIFTSURE racked up 73 miles for every cord that went into the firebox.

Atlanta was one of the South's great railroad terminals; the Georgia Railroad, building west from Augusta, reached the

(Courtesy of the National Archives)

place in 1845, and not long after, the rails of the Macon & Western entered the rapidly growing rail center. The Atlanta & West Point trains also served the town, using Macon & Western tracks from nearby East Point.

The importance of Atlanta as a railroad nerve center and the vital position it occupied in supplying the Confederacy made it a prime target for General Sherman on his famous march through Georgia.

---·---

RAILS AND BULLS

Two yoke of oxen used by the Construction Corps stand beside the partly-completed rolling mill located in Chattanooga, Tennessee; in the left background is the dim profile of Lookout Mountain, famous Civil War landmark.

It appears that the oxen used by the Construction Corps served both under the yoke and the knife and fork, the work teams being slaughtered for food when needed and replaced with other live beef rations on the hoof from the herds of the Army's Commissary. In a post-war letter to General Haupt, E. C. Smeed wrote regarding the Tennessee-Georgia campaigns: "Our land transportation was all done with ox teams, which were drawn from the Commissary and returned to the Commissary when we were out of beef and a new provision return made out for more meat rations."

(Courtesy of the National Archives)

KNIGHTS OF THE HIGH IRON

A crew of the U.S. Military Railroads pose with Engine No. 156, a Baldwin woodburner built in 1864; this engine was reportedly sold to the Mobile & Ohio Railroad when her war duties were over. The monkey wrench and long-spouted oil can held by the civilian railroaders shown in this photo were standard equipment around locomotives until the end of steam.

Engine 156 has an elaborate landscape painted on the side of her oil headlight, and the two boiler check valves indicate she is equipped with both the old crosshead water pump and the new injector; just forward of the boiler checks can be seen the cylinder cock lever, extending down from the hand rail. This lever was connected to a handle in the cab by a rod concealed inside the hollow hand rail.

The old crosshead cold water pumps, which supplied water to the boiler only when the engine was in motion, nearly caused an accident on the Nashville & Chattanooga Railroad shortly after the start of the Civil War. The incident was related by Lafayette Lynch, who started as a brakeman under Supt. Edmund W. Cole in 1854 and worked his way up, becoming a wood passer, a fireman, and finally a locomotive engineer. On the night of the near-accident, Engineer Lynch was in a side track at Raccoon Mountain, just out of Chattanooga, with a Nashville & Chattanooga locomotive named the CUMBERLAND, a Baldwin product of 1853. The water in the boiler got low and Lynch took the CUMBERLAND out onto the main line to pump her up. The engine was a large one for her day, reportedly too heavy for satisfactory operation on the light rails, and her steam was evidently low, for when Lynch pumped the cold water into her boiler, the old girl stalled. A passenger train was about due, but Lynch had no lamp with which to flag the varnished cars and prevent them from crashing into his stalled engine. The quick-witted runner siezed the fireman's tongs, hauled a blazing stick of wood out of the firebox, and ran down the tracks to stop the night passenger train. Fortunately for all concerned, the passenger was late and the old CUMBERLAND raised enough steam to crawl back into the safety of the side track before the over-due train arrived.

(Courtesy of the National Archives)

(Courtesy of the National Archives)

END OF THE LINE

The last ride on the steam cars for many captured Northern soldiers terminated at this station on the Southwestern Railroad in Georgia. The wooden frame structures shown here housed the depot at the station of Andersonville, the infamous Confederate prisoner of war stockade located in Sumter County, Georgia. More than 41,000 Union prisoners were confined here in an area of about 13 acres, sheltered only by open tents. After the War ended, Capt. Henri Wirz, commandant of the Andersonville prison, was executed as a war criminal in the old Capitol Prison in Washington, D.C.

This photo presents an unusually fine view of the old "stringer" type of railroad track in use on many early lines in the South. Ties were laid in the usual manner, and long squared timbers or "stringers" were then placed across them; the iron rails were then spiked to the top surface of the "stringers," as shown here.

TENNESSEE RIVER CROSSING

This historic photograph shows a locomotive and three cars of the United States Military Railroad on the lengthy bridge over the Tennessee River at Loudon, on the East Tennessee & Georgia Railroad. The engine is No. 39, built for the U.S.M.R.R. by Wm. Mason in 1864, bearing Mason's shop No. 150.

The big Loudon bridge had been destroyed earlier in the War, but the road between Chattanooga and Knoxville was in use by the invading Union forces in February of 1864. Supplies and troops using this rail line were ferried across the Tennessee at Loudon until May of 1864, when the bridge shown here was completed. Service over the line was then inaugurated and maintained until August of 1864, when Confederate forces under General Wheeler raided the road and tore up 25 miles of track. The damage was speedily repaired and the road was used until August 28th, 1865, when it was returned to its owners by the Federal Government.

A branch of the East Tennessee & Georgia Railroad was also restored to service and used by the Military Railroad. This road, 27 miles long, left the ET&G main line at Cleveland, Tennessee, and connected with the Western & Atlantic Railroad at Dalton, in north-western Georgia.

Reconstruction of the East Tennessee & Virginia Railroad was ordered by Major General Thomas and the work was commenced north from a point near Knoxville on March 4th, 1865. By April 23rd, the Construction Corps had opened the road to Carter's Station, 110 miles north-east of the Knoxville terminal. The project had been a major task, with 12 miles of track rebuilt, 94 miles of track repaired, and 4,400 lineal feet of bridges reconstructed. The Military Railroad forces also controlled 12 miles of the little Rogersville & Jefferson Railroad, which extended from a junction about 55 miles northeast of Knoxville on the East Tennessee & Virginia Railroad to Rogersville, Tenn.

When General Hood and his hardy Confederates circled to the rear of Sherman's army in October of 1864, they fell upon the Western & Atlantic Railroad, the main supply line of the Union forces in Georgia. Hood's men hit the road in several places, destroying 35½ miles of track and 455 lineal feet of bridges. The major portion of the damaged road lay between Tunnel Hill and Resaca. As soon as Hood moved on,

the repair gangs went into action from both ends of the broken line. Other crews and trains of material were rushed over the ET&G branch from Cleveland to Dalton, and repairs begun in both directions from the Dalton station, located near the center of the wrecked section of the Western & Atlantic. The crews had the road repaired and train service restored between Chattanooga and Atlanta just 13 days after Hood had left the line in smoking ruins.

————————•————————

LOUDON BRIDGE

This view of the Loudon bridge shows the high wooden truss which spanned the main channel of the Tennessee River. The camera, looking east, probably captured this scene on the East Tennessee & Georgia Railroad shortly after the bridge was rebuilt by the Construction Corps for use by the U.S. Military Railroad, and the men pictured on the structure are probably officers and personnel of the task force assigned to rebuild the bridge. When the Fourth Army Corps was moved from Carter's Station to Nashville in 1865, a total of 1,498 cars passed over this bridge on their 373-mile long journey west.

(Courtesy of the National Archives)

(Courtesy of the Norfolk & Western Ry.)

ANTE-BELLUM MOTIVE POWER

Mystery surrounds the actual ownership of the old outside-framed engine ROANOKE, some sources believing her to be one of the early locomotives of the old Virginia & Tennessee Railroad, opened between Lynchburg and Bristol about 1857. At any rate, she is typical of the equipment in use on some Southern railroads at the start of the Civil War.

Very few operating men recorded their experiences on the roads running within the Confederacy, but J. J. Thomas, a long-time locomotive engineer, set down some of the interesting details in his book, "Fifty Years on the Rail," published by the Knickerbocker Press of New York in 1912. Engineer Thomas, a native of Georgia, started his rail career as a brakeman on the old Western & Atlantic Railroad out of Atlanta when it took four days to make a round trip to Chattanooga with a freight train, the crew laying up at night. In 1859 he left the State Road and hired out on the Macon & Western, first as a baggage master and later as a fireman. In 1860 he hired out to Master Mechanic "Uncle Jimmy" Crawford as a switch engineer on the Memphis & Charleston Railroad at Huntsville, Alabama. In January, 1861, he was promoted to road service and took his bride along on a work train tieing up near Iuka, Mississippi. Injured in a derailment in December, 1860, he was off for some time, then was sent into Mississippi with equipment of the Memphis & Charleston being evacuated from Memphis. Thomas later secured a job running an engine on the Southern R.R. of Mississippi, extending from Meridian to Vicksburg, and was at the throttle of the last train into Vicksburg before Grant laid siege to that terminal, remaining there until the siege ended.

Business on the Meridian-Vicksburg road had been very heavy and the motive power was small and inadequate; Thomas recalled being on duty for three days and nights without rest, a man being detailed to see that he did not fall asleep. After being paroled from Vicksburg, Thomas ran between Brandon and Meridian until the advancing Union forces drove him from his job. In March of 1864, he took a job running an engine out of Selma, Alabama, for the Confederate States Government; his run was between Selma and Lime Kiln Station (now Calera) and he moved his wife to the latter place where their first child, J. J. Thomas, Jr., was born. The child later grew up to become Supt. of Motive Power for the Mobile & Ohio Railroad.

Engineer Thomas left the South & North road in the fall of 1864 and took a job running a local freight engine between Selma and Blue Mountain, on the Alabama & Tennessee Rivers Railroad; when Union troops under Wilson raided the road in the spring of 1865, Thomas was put on General Forrest's ordnance train and had a number of close escapes from being captured or shot. Loading his family into a caboose, he helped evacuate rolling stock from Selma to Demopolis, later returning to Uniontown, where he was stationed when the war ended. His experiences during the war included a variety of accidents, collisions, and long hours spent at the throttle, often penniless and frequently hungry.

(Courtesy of National Archives)

RED CLAY HILLS OF GEORGIA

The broken hill country of northern Georgia, former home of the Cherokee Indians, forms the backdrop for this view of the Western & Atlantic Railroad's bridge over the Etowah River. The colorful names of many of the rivers, mountains, and villages in the region are of Cherokee ancestry.

When General Sherman's Yankees marched out of Chattanooga on May Day of 1864, about 25 miles of the north end of the Western & Atlantic, better known as the State Road because of its ownership by the State of Georgia, was held by Union forces and operated as a military rail line, the service extending as far south as Ringgold. South of Ringgold, the road was held by the Confederate Army of Tennessee, led by General Joseph E. Johnston. As the Union troops, some 100,000 strong, swept south along the crooked ribbon of iron, the 45,000 grey-clad sons of the South were forced back in a series of engagements that soaked the red clay with a brighter stain of crimson. General Johnston, knowing he was seriously outnumbered, cautiously retreated along the W&A, destroying the railroad bridges and removing cars and engines as he withdrew.

The Union's Construction Corps kept pace with Sherman's advances and the whistle of Military Railroad engines assured "Uncle Billy" that his needed supplies were close behind. By the 20th day of May, 1864, Federal trains were running to Kingston, and in early June the Construction Corps completed rebuilding of the 600-foot bridge over the Etowah at the location shown in this photo; the job took the experienced veterans about five and a half days. Note the earthwork fortifications thrown up for the defense of this important river crossing.

(Courtesy of AAR)

BUDD CAR ANCESTOR?

This view of the bridge over the Chattahoochee River on the Western & Atlantic Railroad near Atlanta, Georgia, includes a novel piece of railroad equipment operated by the United States Military Railroads. The odd car standing on the bridge was a self-propelled steam coach, used by Military Railroad

officers as an inspection vehicle and as a pay car for distributing wages to the men employed on the widely-scattered operations in the West. A vertical steam boiler located in the front end of the car (shown here at the left) provided steam for a set of engines connected to the wheels of the leading truck. Very little is known about the origin of this car, although it may have come to the Military Railroads from some civilian railroad line.

The bridge over the Chattahoochee was regarded by General Haupt as the most extraordinary feat in military bridge construction that the world had ever seen. It was 780 feet long, over 90 feet high, and was built in 4½ working days with material cut from the stump in the vicinity; the stone piers visible in the photo were the remains of an earlier Western & Atlantic bridge that had been destroyed.

In his memoirs, General Sherman gave credit to W. W. Wright for the success of the rail operations in the campaign to take Atlanta, but neglected to mention Adna Anderson, who had charge of reconstruction of the lines used, or E. C. Smeed, the trusted veteran in charge of bridge work. The Chattahoochee span was one of Smeed's major construction achievements during his long service with the Military Railroads.

MILITARY EXPEDIENT

In their haste to restore the Military Railroad lines, the Construction Corps used whatever material was available to rebuild the destroyed bridges. This view of the trestle across Running Water Ravine on the Nashville & Chattanooga Railroad shows the flimsy nature of the wooden spans thrown up to open the line for military traffic; the remains of the old waterpower mill in the right foreground have probably been partly dismantled to obtain bridge material.

The spindly poles used in the trestle were cut from any available stand of timber near the site, although in some instances the timber had to be hauled from a distance. This Cumberland Mountain trestle near Whiteside, Tennessee, in the Raccoon Range was 780 feet long and 116 feet high in the center of the span. It was rebuilt by the Construction Corps in 1863.

(Courtesy of the National Archives)

SHERMAN'S SOUVENIR

When General William Tecumseh Sherman moved out of Atlanta, Georgia, in November of 1864, he left this ruin behind him. The view shows the remains of the roundhouse located near Foundry and Market Streets, a structure used jointly by the Georgia Railroad and the Atlanta & West Point Railroad.

The engine with outside frames, standing on the turntable, is the O. A. BULL, an Atlanta & West Point 4-4-0 built by Baldwin in May, 1859. In the foreground is another Atlanta & West Point locomotive, the TELEGRAPH. This old 4-4-0 was built by Rogers, Ketchum & Grosvenor in October, 1855, and bore Shop No. 618. She was built for the old Atlanta & LaGrange Railroad, a predecessor of the Atlanta & West Point that was chartered in 1847.

Other locomotives shown in this photograph taken by G. N. Barnard are the E. Y. HILL, M. P. STOVALL, E. L. ELLS-

WORTH, and the HERCULES. The HERCULES belonged to the Georgia Railroad and was built by Norris in 1850; she had 54 inch drivers and was condemned in 1866.

The E. Y. HILL was built by R. Norris in 1852 as the second locomotive on the Atlanta & LaGrange Railroad. She was named in honor of E. Y. Hill, a son of Dr. W. G. Hill; Dr. Hill had gone to Milledgeville, the capitol of Georgia in 1831, to support the incorporation of Franklin, later renamed West Point, and the terminus of the Atlanta & West Point Railroad.

The Georgia Railroad, chartered in 1833, completed its 171 miles of track from Augusta to Atlanta in 1845. Branches ran from Barnett to Washington and from Union Point to Athens; the little Augusta & Milledgeville left the Georgia R.R. main line at Camak and extended to Warrenton. The

Georgia Railroad helped move the First Corps of the Confederacy's Army of Northern Virginia to Atlanta on its way to the Battle of Chickamauga in September of 1863.

When Sherman's Union soldiers moved on Atlanta in 1864, the left wing of the Federal army blocked the Georgia road's line; trains serving the Confederacy from Augusta ran only 96 miles west to Buck Head. On his march to the sea, Sherman desolated the Georgia Railroad from Atlanta to a point where the line crossed the Oconee River east of Madison.

(Courtesy of R. B. Carneal)

PROUD GEORGIAN

The Atlanta & LaGrange Rail Road Company was chartered in December, 1847, but before the road was completed the name was changed to the Atlanta & West Point Railroad. The 80 miles of 5 foot gauge track was opened for service in May, 1854. The road extended from East Point, 6.5 miles south of Atlanta, to West Point, the terminus located on the Chattahoochee River at the Georgia-Alabama border. The road entered Atlanta from East Point over the tracks of the Macon & Western Railroad.

The old 4-4-0 shown here was operated by the Atlanta & West Point and was named the DR. THOMPSON, in honor of Dr. Joseph Thompson, a prominent citizen of Atlanta. The engine was built by the Rogers Locomotive & Machine Works in 1860; note the extremely ornate bell bracket and the typical Rogers fluted sand dome. The oval plaque on the cab panel contains a photograph or a daguerreotype; on one Georgia road each engineer had his own likeness mounted on the cab of his regular locomotive in this manner.

The Atlanta & West Point was closely linked with the Georgia Railroad, another 5 foot gauge line running east from Atlanta to Augusta, where connections were made with the South Carolina Railroad, extending on to Charleston, South Carolina. When Union forces cut the Western & Atlantic line, the Altanta & West Point was the sole rail link between Atlanta and the southwestern regions of the Confederacy. When Sherman marched east from Atlanta, the task of repairing the damaged A&WP was given to Confederate Major Hottel of the Railroad Bureau and the line was placed in limited operation on Jan. 20, 1865.

OLD HERO

The identification caption for this photograph in the catalog of War Department views reads: "Engine 'HERO,' partially destroyed by the Confederates when evacuating Atlanta." The photo was made in 1864 by Photographer George N. Barnard.

The locomotive shown in this view is, in all probability, the old GENERAL of the Western & Atlantic Railroad, and was titled "HERO" by the compiler of the War Department Catalog because of the role the engine played in the raid on the Western & Atlantic by the Union forces led by the mysterious James J. Andrews. The GENERAL was a 4-4-0 type built by Rogers, Ketchum & Grosvenor in 1855, had 15x22 inch cylinders, 60 inch drivers, and was a woodburner carrying about 140 pounds of boiler pressure.

The story of the Andrews raid has been recounted many times and there are various discrepancies in the printed versions. The plan of slipping behind Confederate lines and stealing a train, then cutting the rail lines as the raiders moved toward the Union lines, seems to have originated with Andrews and was authorized by General Ormsby MacKnight Mitchel. Andrews, who apparently served as a spy and perhaps a contraband runner, made one futile attempt but was thwarted when the locomotive engineer on the Western & Atlantic, a Union sympathizer, was found to have been sent off to another section of Confederate rail operations. On the second attempt, Andrews took some Union soldiers along who had civilian experience running locomotives; these engineers were Wilson W. Brown and Wm. J. Knight. The Andrews party slipped through the Rebel lines and boarded a Western & Atlantic train at Marietta, Georgia, on Saturday morning, April 12, 1862. The train was pulled by the engine, GENERAL, Engineer Jeff Cain, and the skipper in charge was Conductor William A. Fuller. Fuller, who was to become the real hero of the ill-fated raid, was 26 years old at the time. A native Georgian, born in Henry County, he had hired out as flagman in 1855 and was promoted to conductor in 1857 at the age of 20.

PERSISTANT SKIPPER

William Allen Fuller, conductor of the stolen train, sparked the pursuit that led to the capture of the Andrews party of Yankee raiders. The 26-year old skipper, toughened by labor

(Courtesy of Louisville & Nashville Railroad)

on his father's farm, was reportedly "strong as an ox and could run like the devil." His stamina and fleetness were a valuable asset as he gave chase to his purloined train.

There were about 3,000 Confederate troops in training at Camp McDonald, opposite the Lacy House at Big Shanty, when the GENERAL was stolen while her crew was taking breakfast, and it was first thought the train had been run off by deserters from the Confederate service; Fuller was quick to perceive that the train thieves were probably Yankee raiders, and sent a telegram to General Danville A. Leadbetter at Chattanooga, warning him to stop the stolen train if Fuller was unable to capture them.

Conductor Fuller died in Atlanta, Georgia, on December 28th, 1905.

167

(Courtesy of the National Archives)

ALLATOONA PASS

When Conductor Fuller and his crew went into the Lacy place to take breakfast at the station called Big Shanty, Georgia, the men of Andrews' party stole the GENERAL and 3 empty box cars and headed north toward Chattanooga. Fuller, Engr. Cain, and Shop Foreman Anthony Murphy took after the stolen train on foot. Murphy, a County Wicklow Irishman, had been aboard the train to examine the pump machinery at the W&A station shown here. Commandeering a track gang's push car, the pursuers soon came upon the old engine, YONAH, at Etowah station. The YONAH, operating on a branch serving the Cooper iron works, was pressed into service and the odds of the race lessened.

The raiders took wood and water at Rogers, and after nerve-wracking delay, met three opposing trains at Kingston and hurried on, Andrews representing the train as a special bearing munitions to Confederate General P. G. T. Beauregard. When the YONAH reached the blocked Kingston yards, Fuller commandeered the WM. R. SMITH, the engine off the Rome Railroad branch passenger train, but the raiders had removed a rail 6 miles north of Kingston and the SMITH was left, Fuller and Murphy running on foot in the wake of the GENERAL. About 2 miles below Adairsville, they met a freight drawn by the TEXAS, a Danforth, Cooke & Co. eight-wheeler, in charge of Engr. Peter Bracken with Fireman Henry Haney and wood-passer Alonzo Martin. The train was side-tracked and the pursuers gave chase aboard the TEXAS, picking up Capt. W. J. Whitsitt of the 1st Georgia Confederate Volunteers and 10 men at Calhoun station. Near Calhoun they also picked up young Ed Henderson, the Dalton telegrapher, who was searching for a break in the wire, which had been cut by the raiders.

REBUILT RACER

After being recaptured from Andrews' raiders, the old GENERAL saw service in the battle of Kennesaw Mountain in the summer of 1864, moving Confederate supplies and wounded. She was damaged when Hood evacuated Atlanta, and was rebuilt in the Western & Atlantic shops in 1868, being given a diamond stack and converted to coal. Her last revenue service was in 1886 and she was taken to Columbus, Ohio, for a reunion of the Grand Army of the Republic in 1888. Rescued from the bone-yard at Vining's Station, Georgia, she was restored in the Nashville, Chattanooga & St. Louis shops at Nashville in 1891 and placed on display in the Union Station, Chattanooga. She was displayed at the Columbian Exposition, Chicago, in 1893; Cotton States & International Exposition in Atlanta, 1895; at Nashville's centennial celebration in 1897; starred in a motion picture under her own steam in 1926, attaining 55 miles per hour; an exhibit at the Baltimore & Ohio's Iron Horse Fair in 1927; at the Century of Progress in Chicago, 1933; at New York World's Fair, 1939-40; at the Chicago Railroad Fair in 1948, and is still on exhibition in Chattanooga. This photo shows the GENERAL in her restored condition, which differs from her original appearance.

(Courtesy of Louisville & Nashville Railroad)

SWIFT PURSUER

This view shows the engine TEXAS of the Western & Atlantic Railroad after she had been rebuilt. The TEXAS, with Engineer Peter Bracken at her throttle, carried Conductor William Fuller and his party in their wild race across the hills of northwestern Georgia in pursuit of James Andrews' group of Yankee raiders aboard the stolen GENERAL.

Andrews, under the guise of carrying a special loaded with powder to General Beauregard, had met the TEXAS at Adairsville and had argued Bracken's crew into sidetracking to let him pass. When the TEXAS proceeded, she was soon met by Murphy and Fuller, who were coming north afoot after being forced to abandon the WM. R. SMITH of the Rome Railroad, the engine commandeered at Kingston along with her engineer, Oliver A. Harbin. The 21 cars behind the TEXAS were shoved into clear at Adairsville and the race between the two engines was on. The TEXAS, built by Danforth, Cooke & Co., was placed in service on the Western & Atlantic in October, 1856. After years of service following Andrews' raid, the TEXAS was placed on exhibit in the basement of the Cyclorama Building in Atlanta's Grant Park, a memorial to the great locomotive chase.

(Courtesy of the Louisville & Nashville Railroad)

TUNNEL HILL

The race between the Yankee raiders aboard the GENERAL and the Southerners in pursuit aboard the TEXAS roared through the red hills of northwest Georgia, the 10 miles between Adairsville and Calhoun being covered in 12 minutes. The raiders attempted to tear up the track behind them, but lack of proper tools and the close proximity of the pursuers hindered their efforts. Andrews' plan to fire the wooden bridges was hampered by a spring rain which drenched the timbers; there is still a controversy in regard to the cars coupled behind the GENERAL, but one of them and possibly more may have been fired and left inside the bridges along the way, to be shoved ahead by the TEXAS to the nearest siding.

The crew on the GENERAL succeeded in taking some wood and water at Green's woodyard before the TEXAS hove into view and put them to flight. The flying engines passed Resaca and Dalton and the smoke from the GENERAL was still drifting from the bore at Tunnel Hill, shown here, as the TEXAS slowed for the rat-hole, expecting to find the track sabotaged within its murky depths. When light from the opposite end reflected on the rails throughout the tunnel, the TEXAS sped on. The chase was nearing its close as the GENERAL roared through Ringgold, her supply of wood exhausted and her water low. The bearings were overheated from lack of lubrication during the chase; as the raiders neared Fowler's place, 2 miles above Ringgold, the engine slowed and the raiders began to leap from the engine and head for the woods. The last men aboard reversed the GENERAL before they jumped, sending her back toward the TEXAS but her steam was low and Pete Bracken reversed his engine and caught the runaway, ending the great locomotive chase. The entire Andrews party was captured within a week, and the leader and seven of his men later were hanged as spies in Atlanta. While very little actual damage was done by the raiders, their audacity stirred the South deeply and feeling against them ran very high.

A better leader might have brought the raid to a different ending. Andrews could have crippled the old YONAH, an important element in the pursuit; his armed men, 21 in number, could have easily overcome the pursuers early in the chase, since they were few in number and their sole arm consisted of a rusty old shotgun snatched up at a depot en route.

IN HOOD'S WAKE

When Confederate General John Bell Hood evacuated Atlanta, the Union forces of General Sherman found this scene of destruction. On the night of August 31st, 1864, Hood's troops marched out of the beleaguered city under a pall of smoke and flames. Thunderous explosions rent the skies over Atlanta as 28 cars loaded with ammunition were fired by the retreating troops. This photograph, credited to the noted Federal photographer George N. Barnard, shows the remains of General Hood's munition trains and the gaunt chimneys marking the ruins of the Schofield Rolling Mill. More than 50 freight cars also went up in flames that night and the crews of the Western & Atlantic Railroad were instructed to render their remaining locomotives useless; among the engines left behind in Atlanta were the GENERAL of Andrews' raid fame, the MISSOURI, and the N. C. MONROE.

In an attempt to evacuate the Confederate wounded from the doomed city, the Confederate officer in charge loaded them aboard a passenger train and headed them south toward Macon behind the locomotive DISPATCH. This special loaded with casualties was apparently started without the knowledge of the Macon & Western dispatcher; about 2 miles north of Barnesville the DISPATCH plowed head-on into the engine GOVERNOR and her train of commissary supplies. More than 30 were killed, many more seriously injured, and both locomotives severely damaged. In addition, 3 box cars and a passenger coach were demolished, a serious blow to a road already hampered by a shortage of rolling stock and motive power.

(Courtesy of the National Archives)

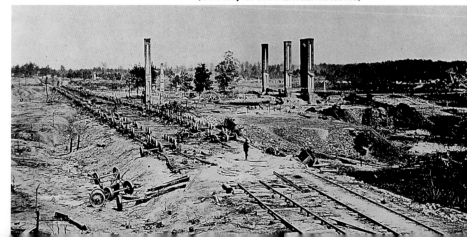

LAST REUNION

These seven veterans of the Andrews raid met for the last time in the National Cemetery at Chattanooga in September of 1906, and are shown here grouped in front of the monument erected by the State of Ohio in 1891; the graves of Andrews and seven of his raiders who were executed lie behind this memorial.

In the front row, left to right, are John R. Porter, who outlived all of the raiding party and died at the age of 85 in 1923; William Knight, one of the locomotive engineers in the Andrews party who ran the stolen GENERAL; Jacob Parrott, who was the first recipient of the Congressional Medal of Honor, awarded for his role in the raid; Anthony Murphy, the Western & Atlantic foreman of machinery and motive power who accompanied Conductor Fuller in pursuit of the raiders; and Daniel A. Dorsey, another of Andrews' men. Standing at

left in the rear is William Bensinger, one of the raiders, and at right is Henry Haney, who outlived all the participants in the thrilling railroad chase.

Henry Haney was 15 years old when the raid took place, and was firing for Engineer Peter Bracken on the TEXAS when she raced after the stolen GENERAL. His father, Tom Haney, was a blacksmith employed in the Atlanta shops of the Western & Atlantic.

Of the raiders in this photo, Knight, Porter, and Dorsey were among the eight members of Andrews' party who escaped from the Confederate prison in Atlanta on October 16th, 1862. Porter and Corporal Martin Hawkins did not actually participate in the locomotive race, having overslept and missed the train when the raiders boarded it at Marietta, Georgia, on that rainy April morning. Both men joined the Confederate Army to escape detection, as previously planned, but were ferreted out and thrown into prison with their comrades. Privates William Bensinger and Jacob Parrott were among the group of six raiders who were paroled by the Confederate authorities at City Point, Virginia, on March 17th, 1863.

Anthony Murphy, the Irish shop foreman, had started his career as an apprentice machinist in Trenton, New Jersey, at the age of 18. After 3 years there, he spent a year in the Erie Railway's shops at Pierpont, New York, and another year in the Pittsburg shops of the Pennsylvania Railroad. Murphy moved to Georgia in 1854, where he served the Western & Atlantic Railroad as a machinist, locomotive engineer, and finally a foreman of machinery under Superintendent John S. Rowland and Master of Machinery Flynn. He married Adelia McConnell, an Atlanta belle noted for her charm and beauty, and had gone to Pennsylvania to recruit mechanics for the Western & Atlantic a short time before the Civil War began.

172

LAST TRAIN

This photo is reputed to show the last train to depart from Atlanta before General Wm. T. Sherman laid waste to the Georgia rail terminal on the eve of his famous march to the sea. The car tops are piled high with the baggage of the refugees fleeing from the doomed city. Sherman had forced Hood out of Atlanta by striking severe blows at the rail lines which supplied the Confederate defenders. In July of 1864, he had sent General Lovell H. Rousseau's cavalry on a lightning raid through the hills of upper Alabama; this force hit the Alabama & Tennessee Rivers Railroad at Talladega, then moved south to the more important Montgomery & West Point. The Union raiders wrecked about 30 miles of track between Cheraw and Opelika, tore up some of the Columbus branch, then rode northward.

Later in July, Union Generals Stoneman and McCook led their columns of blue-coated cavalry in a sweep south of Atlanta along the Macon & Western Railroad. This force cut the Macon & Western line at Lovejoy's Station and galloped on to the banks of the Ocmulgee River opposite Macon. Here Stoneman's party swung east along the Central Railroad of Georgia, burning the Walnut Creek and Oconee bridges. Their richest prize was found at Gordon, where the Central of Georgia's branch line from Eatonton and Milledgeville joined the main stem. The yards at Gordon held a quantity of Western & Atlantic rolling stock that had been sent south for safety in the face of Sherman's advance; the raiders destroyed over 45 freight and passenger cars and damaged four locomotives of the Western & Atlantic that reposed in this apparently secure place of refuge. The line between Oconee and Macon was out of service for a month as a result of the raid.

Although most of the raiding party was surrounded and captured, they staged one of the spectacular train wrecks that frequently marked railroad operations during the War. Not far from Griswoldville the raiders captured a 27-car freight train. The cars were burned and the locomotive was uncoupled and turned loose down the main line with its throttle peeled wide open. The wild engine roared into the Griswoldville station and struck the rear end of a passenger train loaded with refugees. Fortunately, the rear coach was an empty and although it was shattered and the cars ahead of it damaged, none of the passengers were seriously injured.

ATLANTA YARDS

A locomotive and troop-laden cars appear in this view of the Atlanta rail yards under Federal occupation.

(Courtesy of Library of Congress)

SCRAP IRON

Union forces under General Sherman are shown here in 1864 as they demolished transportation facilities in Atlanta. The crew in the foreground are twisting rails by means of clamps and levers, after the worn rails have been heated on a pyre of burning ties; this scene was probably taken in the yards of the Western & Atlantic Railroad.

The loss of Confederate rolling stock when the city was evacuated in the face of Sherman's siege was a heavy blow to the Southern cause. After the smoke of flaming destruction had cleared a bit, the blame for the loss of this equipment was placed on Hood's Chief Quartermaster, Lieutenant Colonel McMicken. In a message to General Braxton Bragg, Hood stated the priceless ammunition, cars, and locomotives were lost through McMicken's "wanton neglect," adding that he had information that indicated McMicken had become so addicted to drink that he was unable to properly attend his duties. A Court of Inquiry held later supported Hood's accusations and considered the Chief Quartermaster "highly culpable," guilty of failure to comply with repeated instructions to have the trains ready to move from the doomed city, and equally guilty of not having issued proper instructions for the evacuation of supplies and equipment to the Atlanta railroad agents and officers.

When Sherman moved out toward Savannah in November of '64, he ordered the Western & Atlantic torn up to protect his rear, and the track from Atlanta to the Etowah River crossing, 46 miles, was destroyed. In addition, 16 miles of track was taken up between Resaca and Dalton, Georgia, and the rails removed to Chattanooga. Major General Thomas later ordered the State Road repaired, and the Construction Corps laid 66 miles of track, repaired an additional 36 miles, and rebuilt many destroyed bridges; this work was accomplished between May 10th and July 4th, 1865. On September 25, 1865, the Western & Atlantic Railroad was returned to the control of the State of Georgia, the original owners of the line, thus ending its turbulent existence as a Civil War carrier.

FLORIDA METROPOLIS

This view shows the depot of the Florida, Atlantic & Gulf Central Railroad at Jacksonville during the Civil War era. Connecting with the Pensacola & Georgia R.R. at Lake City, the road formed the eastern part of a line from Jacksonville to Tallahassee and St. Marks. At Baldwin, Florida, west of Jacksonville, the Florida, Atlantic & Gulf Central crossed the Florida Railroad, which ran from Fernandina on the Atlantic seaboard to Cedar Key, located on the Gulf shore of Tampa Bay.

When Admiral Dupont's Federal fleet recaptured Fort Clinch at Fernandina in March of 1862, Captain Drayton noted a Florida Railroad train evacuating the city with a long string of cars; the railroad ran along the shore line for about 4 miles, and Drayton ordered Lt. Stearns of the OTTOWA to stop the train. The gunboat was no match in speed for the locomotive and Stearns ordered his guns to open fire. One shot struck a flat car and killed two men; the train crew cut off part of their long drag and ran off with the head end to a position of safety inland. Many frightened passengers leaped from the train and hid in the bushes during the shelling, among them the president of the road, ex-United States Senator David L. Yulee.

(Courtesy of the National Archives)

175

SMOKING RUBBLE   (Courtesy of the Library of Congress)

This view shows the remains of the Western & Atlantic Railroad structure called the "car sheds" in Atlanta after it was destroyed by the Union forces under General W. T. Sherman shortly before they evacuated the Georgia rail center.

Similar scenes of smoking ruins marked the trail of the Federal raid through the South led by Major General James Harrison Wilson early in 1865. Wilson, commanding the Cavalry Corps, Division of the Mississippi, organized his raiding party near Waterloo and Gravelly Ford, located in northwestern Alabama; the force consisted of 12,000 horsemen, 1,500 dismounted men, and three artillery outfits. The latter was composed of the 18th Battery, Indiana Light Artillery; Chicago Board of Trade Battery, Illinois Light Artillery; and Battery I, 4th U.S. Artillery.

The force crossed the Tennessee River on March 18th, 1865, travelling light and intending to mount the 1,500 foot troops with horses procured along the way. Each mounted trooper carried 24 lbs. of grain, 100 rounds of ammunition, 5 days' rations, and 2 spare horseshoes. Pack animals carried hard tack, sugar, salt, and coffee, and 250 wagons in the supply train hauled extra ammunition and supplies.

On March 30th the invaders were in the suburbs of Birmingham and destroyed five iron works around nearby Montevallo. By the 2nd of April, the main force captured Selma, Alabama, a major Confederate rail terminal. The roundhouses of the Alabama & Tennessee Rivers Railroad and the Alabama & Mississippi Rivers Railroad were both destroyed, along with five locomotives, shop machinery, and about 90 freight and passenger cars.

The Yankees hit Montgomery on April 12th, destroying several locomotives and steamboats, an armory, and several foundries.

Aided by beautiful spring weather, the troopers arrived at Columbus, Georgia, on Easter Sunday and after a night battle, captured that important city. Columbus was served by the Muscogee Railroad, running east to a junction with the Southwestern Railroad at Butler; from Girard, on the opposite banks of the Chattahoochee, the Mobile & Girard ran southwest to Union Springs and a branch of the Montgomery & West Point ran northwest to Opelika, Alabama. The raiders burned two roundhouses and two machine shops in the Columbus-Girard terminals, burned the river bridges, and destroyed about 15 locomotives and nearly 100 freight and passenger cars. In addition, the destruction included about 160,000 bales of cotton, foundries, arms factories, shipyards, and the newly-completed Confederate ironclad ram, the JACKSON.

North of Columbus, Wilson's raiders hit West Point, on the Georgia-Alabama line; fire and the sledge hammer destroyed 20 locomotives, including all 19 engines in good condition belonging to the Montgomery & West Point Railroad; about 350 loaded cars were also put to the torch. The raiders captured the vital Macon terminal on March 20th, 1865, and were occupying that strategic location when the news was received that General Johnston had surrendered to General Sherman and that the war was at an end.

176

'WAY DOWN YONDER

When the city of New Orleans was captured by Commodore Farragut's invasion fleet in April of 1862, the prizes taken included the 80 miles of 5-foot 6-inch gauge track and other properties of the New Orleans, Opelousas & Great Western Railroad, extending from Algiers, opposite New Orleans, to Brashear City on Berwick's Bay, Louisiana. The road had 12 locomotives in service when placed under the control of Colonel J. McMillan of the 21st Indiana Regiment on May 1st, 1862; other equipment included the sidewheeler CERES, used as a ferry across the Mississippi, and one freight barge, two other barges having been burned at the time of the invasion to prevent them from falling into Yankee hands.

By Order No. 20, Major General Benj. F. Butler returned the road to the owners on May 3, 1862, and service was resumed May 8th, the line being required to transport food supplies needed in New Orleans. Operations were disrupted on May 26th when a force of Confederate Rangers from St. Martinsville, under orders of the general commanding the 9th Brigade, Louisiana Militia, captured a train at Bayou Boeuf. The raiders boldly steamed east to Jefferson Station, near Avondale, where they proceeded to tear up the track almost under the noses of the Union forces quartered in Algiers. Reversing their woodburner, they retreated west and burned the bridges at Des Allemands, Lafourche, and Bayou Boeuf as they went. Three locomotives and about half of the road's rolling stock remained in Confederate hands on the western section of the line between Bayou Boeuf and Berwick's Bay.

Union forces commanded by Colonel S. Thomas of the 8th Vermont Regiment took over the eastern portion of the road on July 1, 1862, and resumed operations from Algiers to Des Allemands, 32 miles.

The view on the following pages shows the Algiers terminal while under Federal control, the photograph reportedly taken in 1864. At the left is the CHRISTOPHER ADAMS, JR., a 24 ton engine built by Rogers, Ketchum & Grosvenor in 1853, Shop No. 421; she had 12½x22 inch cylinders and 72 inch drivers, and was named in honor of the first president of the New Orleans, Opelousas & Great Western. The engine at right is the LAFOURCHE, built for the road by the Taunton Locomotive Works in May, 1859, and placed in service on September 15th of that year. The LAFOURCHE weighed 20 tons, had 16x22 inch cylinders and 60 inch drivers. In this photo the tender of the LAFOURCHE and the coach behind her are both lettered "U.S.M.R.R.," but the road was never actually under the United States Military Railroads' control, being operated by the Quartermaster Department under the military Department of the Gulf.

(Courtesy of the Smithsonian Institution)

(Courtesy of Chas. E. Fisher)

WESTERN WOODBURNER

New Jersey Locomotive & Machine Company of Paterson, New Jersey, turned out Engine 150 for the U.S. Military Railroads in 1864. During the entire war, the engines purchased or captured and under control of the U.S. Military Railroads totaled 419, according to Genl. McCallum's reports; these figures probably include a number of new locomotives ordered shortly before the war ended. These new engines were delivered to the Army but were stored around Manchester, Virginia, and not used; they were later sold by Government order.

The demand for skilled locomotive engineers was great, and experienced men were recruited from all over the North to handle the throttles on the military lines. The engineers ranked at the top of the operating crews' wage scale on most Northern railroads, their pay averaging $3.00 per day; firemen drew $1.75, conductors about $1.66, and brakemen about $1.33.

General McCallum, who served as General Manager of the U.S. Military Railroads, had set an example of typical labor relations when he was in charge of the Erie Railroad in

1854; his strict operating rules were not too objectionable, but he inaugurated the "black list," the policy of notifying other railroads whenever an Erie employee was discharged, and this caused a series of strikes which helped force the road into receivership.

As a result of such oppression, magnified during the War, the first of the great railroad labor unions was founded in 1863; originally called the Brotherhood of the Footboard by the few men under W. D. Robinson at their first meeting in Marshall, Michigan, this organization became the Brotherhood of Locomotive Engineers.

WAR IN THE WEST

As the flames of war swept Kentucky and Tennessee in the fall of 1861, Colonel (later General) Ormsby Mitchel proposed a raid from the Blue Grass State to the line of the East Tennessee & Virginia Railroad near Knoxville, Tenn., proposing to burn the long bridges near that terminal and thus cut the main east-west rail line of the Confederacy. This raid was opposed by Federal Commander Wm. T. Sherman and was called off. In November of 1861, inspired by hazy rumors that Union forces under General Thomas would come to their aid, a number of loyal East Tennesseans launched a bridge-burning campaign in southeastern Tennessee and northeastern Alabama. They fired a number of railroad spans, but the Union aid never came and the bridge-burners were hunted down by the Confederates; some were shot, others tried and hung, and many suspects were thrown into prison.

In March of 1862, Mitchel moved south from Shelbyville and attacked Huntsville, Alabama, on the Memphis & Charleston Railroad. Artillery, with cavalry support, cut the railroad east of town, leading to Chattanooga; the attack came early in the morning of April 11, 1862. A rebel train heading east was fired on but managed to escape; a following train was hit by artillery fire, killing the engineer and disabling the locomotive. By 6:00 A.M. Mitchel's command, consisting of Turchin's brigade, Kennett's cavalry, and Simonson's battery, was in possession of Huntsville. They bagged about 200 prisoners, 15 locomotives, and a large number of freight and passenger cars,

and captured intact the enginehouse and turntable, telegraph office, wood and water facilities, and other terminal structures.

Mitchel appointed Mr. Larcombe, the railroad telegrapher at Huntsville, as Superintendent of the captured section of road; Larcombe reportedly was a strong Union sympathizer. At 6:00 P.M. on the day Huntsville was captured, a train steamed west bearing troops of the 24th Illinois under command of the colorful Capt. J. B. Turchin. Early on the morning of April 12th, this force captured the Memphis & Charleston station of Decatur, driving off the Confederate defenders and extinguishing the burning railroad bridge which had been fired by the rebels.

When dawn broke on the morning of April 12th, another train chuffed east from Huntsville, loaded with Colonel Sill's brigade; General Mitchel rode in the cab of the locomotive and Col. Sill rode on a flat car bearing an artillery piece which was shoved ahead of the engine. The rail-borne invaders moved cautiously east for about 70 miles, constantly watching for an ambush; meeting no resistance, they boldly steamed in Stevenson, Alabama, where they captured the town and 5 good locomotives. The force moved east about 7 miles to Widden's Creek, where they halted and set up a defense, having successfully cut the main Confederate rail line between Virginia and the Mississippi.

This post-war view shows the Memphis & Charleston Railroad terminus at Memphis, Tennessee.

KEY CITY RAIL YARDS

This rare view shows the railroad yards in Vicksburg, Mississippi, after the surrender of the Confederates on July 4th, 1863. The shattered buildings show the effects of the heavy bombardment by the Federal forces under General U. S. Grant during the lengthy siege before the Confederate defenders were finally starved out.

Vicksburg, located at the junction of the Yazoo and Mississippi rivers, was the last major Confederate stronghold on the Mississippi and when the city fell, the river was in Federal hands, splitting the Confederacy in twain.

Vicksburg was served by the Vicksburg & Meridian Railroad, a 5-foot gauge rail line, 140 miles long, running east from the Mississippi port to Meridian, near the Alabama border. The Vicksburg & Meridian was formed in 1856 by a consolidation of the Vicksburg & Jackson Railroad, chartered in 1835, and the Southern Railroad of Mississippi, chartered in 1837. The road was opened from Vicksburg east to Jackson in 1841, and was extended to Meridian in 1860; a short line, known as the Raymond Branch or Raymond Railroad, extended 7 miles from Bolton Depot to Raymond and was completed in 1850 but later torn up.

At Jackson, Mississippi, the Vicksburg & Meridian connected with the New Orleans, Jackson & Great Northern Railroad, which ran south to New Orleans, and the Mississippi Central Railroad, the latter forming an important connecting link north through Canton and Grenada to the Memphis & Charleston and other lines in western Tennessee.

At Meridian, the Vicksburg & Meridian joined the big Mobile & Ohio Railroad, a major north-south Confederate traffic artery. The Mobile & Ohio, successor to the Mobile & Tennessee Railroad, was started in 1849 and the 472 miles of 5-foot gauge road was completed from Mobile, Alabama, to Columbus, Kentucky, in September, 1859.

During the War, the Confederate Government made efforts to complete an east-west connection from Meridian to the lines in central Alabama; the Northeast & Southwest Railroad built east from Meridian to Reagan, Alabama, and the Alabama & Mississippi Rivers Railroad attempted to connect Reagan with Selma, Alabama, via McDowell's Bluff and Demopolis, but the union failed. The capture of New Orleans caused the loss of priceless rails destined for the project, and what work was completed was hampered when the planters recalled their slaves from the grading jobs to work in the harvest.

————•————

SOUTHERN SHORT LINE

The West Feliciana Railroad, 27.5 miles long, was a standard gauge line extending from Bayou Sara, Louisiana, to Woodville, Mississippi. The road was chartered in March, 1831, and was opened for traffic in 1835, operating over the old strap-iron rail then in common use. The road played only a very minor role in the Civil War; it later became a part of the Yazoo & Mississippi Valley, which in turn passed under Illinois Central control. The old Norris engine shown here is the G. H. GORDON, but the number, 200, was probably a Y&MV number, as the West Feliciana operated in 1876 with only two locomotives.

(Courtesy of Norfolk & Western Railway)

A LINE DIVIDED

While the eastern end of the New Orleans, Opelousas & Great Western was being operated by the Yankees, the western section of the road was used by the gray-clad ranks of the Confederacy. This situation existed until the fore part of November, 1862, when the Union forces launched a drive to recapture the entire line. A special train moved west from Algiers, carrying cannon mounted on flat cars and a strong escort of sol-

diers. By means of temporary bridges hastily thrown across the bayous, the Federals moved over the road, driving the Confederates before them; although the Rebs destroyed railroad buildings and rolling stock and damaged two locomotives, the Yankees gained control of the entire 80 miles of track by November 12th, 1862, and held the line until it was restored to the owners on February 1st, 1866.

Under Union control, two locomotives of the road were shipped up-river to the Memphis & Little Rock Railroad, along with a number of cars, to operate under the U.S. Military Railroad control on the line between Duvall's Bluff and Little Rock, Arkansas, a distance of 49 miles. The two NOO&GW engines sent there were the CHRISTOPHER ADAMS, JR., and the OPELOUSAS, the latter being a 4-4-0 built by Baldwin in 1853, Shop No. 512.

A third locomotive of the New Orleans, Opelousas & Great Western reportedly was shipped off to Texas by the Federal forces, along with a number of cars, to operate on the Brazos Santiago & Brownsville Railroad. This engine, named the GREAT WESTERN, was a 4-4-0 built by Rogers, Ketchum & Grosvenor in 1854.

A list of motive power to be turned over to the Company on February 15th, 1866, by Chief Acting Quartermaster J. Chandler, Department of the Gulf, included the NOO&GW engines TEXAS, NACHITOCHES, TERREBONNE, NEW ORLEANS, SABINE, and TIGER, all 4-4-0 types built by Niles & Co. of Cincinnati, Ohio, except the TIGER, a Niles & Co. 0-4-0; also returned were the former NOO&GW locomotives ST. MARY, LAFOURCHEE, and NEW IBERIA, three 4-4-0's built by Taunton in 1859. In addition, the Government list included the COL. HOLABIRD, a 4-4-0 built under Federal supervision in the Algiers Shops during the occupation.

The upper view shows the CHRISTOPHER ADAMS, JR., while the lower view shows two of the roads' unidentified woodburners at Algiers, probably a Niles machine at left and a Taunton at right.

(Courtesy of Thomas Norrell)

OCCUPATION PRODUCT

While the Union forces were in control of Louisiana, the shops of the New Orleans, Opelousas & Great Western Railroad turned out this 4-4-0 woodburner, erected under the supervision of the U.S. Quarter Master Department. The engine was named the COL. HOLABIRD and was included in the list of locomotives to be returned to the management of the road prepared by J. Chandler, Chief Acting Q.M., Department of the Gulf, in February, 1866. In January, 1869, the General Superintendent of the New Orleans, Opelousas & Western listed and named 10 engines in use on the road; included in this roster was a 1st class locomotive, 22 tons weight, named the W. G. HEWES. The roster states that this locomotive was built in the Company's shops (Algiers) by the United States Government, and was first used in May, 1865. There is a strong possibility that the W. G. HEWES, named in honor of a former NOO&GW president, was the former COL. HOLABIRD and that the Southerners who ran the line had simply renamed the engine, eliminating the Yankee officer's name in favor of that of a former railroad official.

Yankee officials had the equipment lettered "U.S.M.R.R.," but the line was never under control of General McCallum's operations.

Rebel troops and sympathizers preyed on the road during the Federal occupation. When an east-bound train headed in at Boutte station for a meet with a west-bound scheduled train, Confederates opened a heavy fire from ambush on the Union guards aboard, killing about 15 and wounding more. Although the train carried a 12-pound artillery piece on a flat car, the concealed rebels poured in such a heavy fire that the entire Yankee force was in danger of being wiped out. The open stub switches at either end of the siding had the train effectively trapped, but Pvt. Lewis Ingalls of the 8th Vermont Infantry, one of the train guards, ran ahead and lined the switch, allowing the engineer to run the train out of the ambuscade; Ingalls was wounded but recovered.

In another instance, an engineer with Confederate leanings halted his train in a swampy region in the black of night and deserted the engine. A following section crashed into the standing train, killing a number of Yankee troops being moved over the road and injuring many others.

(Upper photo, courtesy of Chas. E. Fisher)
(Lower photo, courtesy of Thomas Norrell)

(Courtesy of the National Archives)

LAST STOP ON THE LONG ROAD

As April's greenery spread over the Virginia countryside, the ragged and hungry Confederate soldiers of Robert E. Lee straggled into camp in the vicinity of Appomattox Courthouse. The star of the Confederacy was waning as the battle-scarred troopers went into bivouac; Petersburg and Richmond had fallen and a special train had carried President Jefferson Davis out of the capitol to avoid capture by the advancing forces commanded by General U. S. Grant. In the face of this gloomy situation, Lee and his staff clung to one faint hope. The supply trains Lee had ordered moved to Amelia Courthouse to await his arrival had been ordered on to Richmond via the Richmond & Danville Railroad to aid in the evacuation; the supplies had not been left at Amelia, but through a stupid blunder had been carried into Richmond and lost to the enemy. Now another convoy of supply trains was moving over the South Side Railroad and they held forth a promise of at least temporary relief.

These trains began to roll into Appomattox Station early in morning of April 8th, 1865, and eager Confederate soldiers, many of them unarmed, began the welcome task of unloading them. The job was suddenly interrupted by hoof-beats and the crackle of carbine fire. A large force of Sheridan's Union cavalry, led by Major General George A. Custer, swooped down on the scene and routed the Confederates. With the vital supply trains in Union hands, Lee's last hope went glimmering and the end came on Palm Sunday, April 9th, 1865. In the neat brick McLean house located at Appomattox Courthouse, Lee signed the terms of surrender to Grant at 3:30 P.M. and the bloody conflict was near its close.

This photograph, from a negative made by Timothy H. O'Sullivan, shows the South Side Railroad track at Appomattox Station, about 96 miles west of Petersburg and about 3 miles from Appomattox Courthouse. The car wheels in the ditch mark the remains of Lee's lost supply trains. The rough track and worn rails are typical of the condition of railroads throughout the South after the War Between the States.

Lincolns Last Train Ride

(Courtesy of Southern Railway)

LINCOLN'S PRIVATE CAR

The ornate coach shown here carried the remains of the martyred president on their last journey from Washington to
Springfield, Illinois, after he was shot by James Wilkes Booth
in Ford's Theater on the fateful night of April 14th, 1865. The
inscription on this photo reads: "Car Built For President
Abraham Lincoln. First used for carrying his body to Springfield, Ill. B. P. Lamison, Supt. Car Dept., U.S. Military R.R.s
of Virginia. W. H. H. Price, Foreman in charge of construction
of car. Alexandria, Va. 1863."

The coach was mounted on four sets of four-wheeled
trucks and the exterior woodwork was a rich chocolate brown.
A side panel between the windows carried the lettering,
"UNITED STATES," and beneath this was an oval plaque
with a fancy reproduction of the nation's coat of arms. The
interior of the car was divided into a center stateroom, a par-
lor, and a drawing room, the latter two connected by an aisle
passing along one side of the coach. The interior walls were
finely upholstered from seat rails to head lining, the upper
deck painted white, and the panels displayed the coats of arms
of the various states. Four lounges, two exceptionally long to
accommodate Lincoln's height, could be opened out to serve
as beds at night.

The festoons of black crepe and the white-gloved honor
guard with black arm-bands of mourning indicate that this
photograph was taken while the car was being used for Lincoln's funeral coach on the sad trip to his old home in Springfield.

186

LINCOLN'S LAST RIDE

The mortal remains of the martyred Abraham Lincoln were solemnly placed in the special car built for his use by the Car Department of the United States Military Railroads and the Lincoln funeral train pulled out of Washington, D.C., at 8:00 A.M. on April 21st, 1865. The funeral train consisted of nine cars, bearing the body of President Lincoln, an honor guard, and a large group of mourners, including many high-ranking officers of the Government and the armed services. The Baltimore & Ohio Railroad handled the funeral special to Baltimore, arriving at the Camden Station at 10:00 A.M. The casket containing the body was carried to the rotunda of the Merchants Exchange for display to the throngs of mourners. Later in the day the remains was moved to the Howard Street Station of the Northern Central Railroad and at 3:00 P.M. the funeral special steamed slowly away on the Northern Central tracks to Harrisburg, Pennsylvania, arriving there at 8:00 P.M.

At Harrisburg, the casket was carried to the State Capitol and placed on display in the hall of the House of Representatives, remaining there overnight. At 10:00 A.M. on April 22nd, the body was taken back to the funeral car and at 12:00 Noon the funeral special left for Philadelphia on the Pennsylvania Railroad. The somber train was hauled by Pennsylvania Railroad's Engine 331, shown here heavily festooned with the black crepe of mourning. The funeral engine was in charge of Engineer J. E. Miller and the train was skippered by Conductor George Phillips.

A special train, consisting of Engine 286 and one coach, preceded the funeral special over the road by 10 minutes to insure that all was well. Aboard the pilot special were Pennsylvania Railroad's General Superintendent Enoch Lewis, Philadelphia Division Superintendent G. C. Franciscus, Train Master W. F. Lockard, and Road Foreman of Engines Samuel Blair.

(Courtesy of H. L. Broadbelt Collection of Baldwin Loco. Works Negatives)

(Courtesy of H. L. Broadbelt Collection of Baldwin Loco. Works Negatives)

FUNERAL SPECIAL IN PENNSYLVANIA

The Lincoln funeral train is shown here behind Pennsylvania Railroad's Engine 331, reportedly near the West Philadelphia Station. The run over the Pennsylvania's tracks from Harrisburg ended at the Broad Street Station of the Philadelphia, Wilmington & Baltimore Railroad in Philadelphia at 4:00 P.M. The remains of the President were reverently escorted to historic old Independence Hall and placed on display there. In Philadelphia, as in all other cities along the route of the sad train, signs of mourning were prominently displayed. Black crepe draped many buildings and crowds of mourners and the curious lined the streets to witness the processions which escorted the casket to the various places where it was exhibited. Country villages turned out to honor the deceased Chief Executive and farm folk lined the right-of-way to glimpse the funeral train as it steamed through the April sunshine.

The special chuffed out of Philadelphia's Kensington Station at 4:00 A.M. on the morning of April 24th, running over the Philadelphia & Trenton Railroad to Trenton, New Jersey.

The train moved over the Camden & Amboy Railroad from Trenton to New Brunswick and from there to Jersey City it ran over the line of the New Jersey Railroad & Transportation Company, arriving at 10:00 A.M. The casket was escorted across to New York's Debrosses Street ferry landing and from there it was taken to a place of honor at the City Hall.

The funeral car was ferried across from Jersey City and coupled into a train of the Hudson River Railroad; the solemn special rolled out of the station at 30th Street at 4:15 P.M. on the 25th of April. The oil lamp of the locomotive cast its yellow glow against the dark of the spring night as the train rumbled north along the waters of the Hudson. The stations along the way loomed and faded as the sorrowing special retraced the route used by Lincoln on his way to Washington for his first inauguration in February of 1861.

Above Peekskill, the grey battlements of West Point topped the bluffs across the Hudson. Within the stone walls of the Military Academy had gathered many students who later became officers in the armies of the North and the South, men who were destined to play important roles in the National Tragedy now culminated in the silent form lying cold in the casket of the funeral special.

The Lincoln train steamed on through Fishkill, Poughkeepsie, and Rhinebeck, pulling into East Albany at 10:55 P.M. Here the body of the martyred President was removed and ferried across the Hudson to Albany and a place of honor in the State Capitol. The train was run on up to Troy and over the bridge there, then moved to the station of the old New York Central Railroad in Albany.

The funeral special moved west out of Albany at 4:00 P.M. on April 26th, running over the New York Central lines through Schenectady and Rochester. It arrived in Buffalo, New York, at 7:00 A.M. on April 27th, and the remains were carried to St. James Hall for display during the day.

———————•———————

RAIL-BORNE CORTEGE

Pennsylvania Railroad's Engine 331, with Engineer J. E. Miller at the throttle, is shown here alongside the depot in Harrisburg, Pennsylvania, ready to pull out on the journey to Philadelphia. The car next to the locomotive is a typical Pennsylvania Railroad baggage car of the Civil War era.

(Courtesy of the Pennsylvania Railroad)

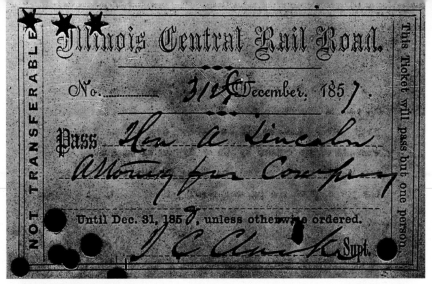

LINCOLN'S PASS

Shown here is the pass issued to Abraham Lincoln when he was employed as an attorney for the Illinois Central R.R. in 1857-58. Lincoln also served in a trial on behalf of the Rock Island in the Mississippi River bridge case, and as President of the United States, he signed the bill which created the first transcontinental railroad and designated the terminus of the Pacific Railroad. He was a firm advocate of rail transport and believed a transcontinental line would help bind the western regions to the Union cause.

(Courtesy of Illinois Central Railroad)

(Courtesy of Dr. S. R. Wood)

FUNERAL TRAIN POWER IN OHIO

The train bearing the body of the martyred president steamed out of Buffalo, New York, at 10:00 P.M. on April 27th, 1865. It rode the rails of the Buffalo & State Line Railroad to the Pennsylvania border and was then turned over to the Erie & North East Railroad for movement to Erie, Pennsylvania. At that point the Cleveland, Painesville & Ashtabula Railroad took over and delivered the train into Cleveland, Ohio, at 7:00 A.M. on April 28th. The casket was removed at the Euclid Street Station and was displayed throughout the day to throngs of mourners in a temporary structure located in a park on Superior Street.

At midnight, the funeral special eased out of the Euclid Street Station on the tracks of the Cleveland, Columbus & Cincinnati Railroad, bound for Columbus, Ohio. The engine assigned to this run was No. 15 of the C.C.&C.R.R., a 4-4-0 named the NASHVILLE. She was built by the Cuyahoga Steam Furnace Company of Cleveland in 1852. Draped with black crepe and crepe-bordered flags, she carried a large framed portrait of Lincoln on her pilot beam and smaller photos mounted between her high drivers. Note the very unusual application of her whistle to the top of her bell bracket; the bracket was evidently hollow and connected to the boiler by a port in the base of the bell mounting. The original photo, copied by railroad historian Dr. S. R. Wood, was apparently taken at the roundhouse before the funeral special left Cleve-Westfall, in cab window.

The Lincoln funeral special arrived in Columbus at 7:00 A.M. on April 29th and the remains were carried to the Ohio State Capitol building and placed on display in the rotunda until evening.

The Cleveland, Columbus & Cincinnati was chartered in 1845 and the first through trains from Cleveland, on Lake Erie, were run through to Columbus, Ohio, on February 22nd, 1851. The distance covered by the road between these two cities was 138 miles. The road acquired 50 miles of track between Delaware and Springfield, Ohio, in 1861 by purchase from the Springfield, Mt. Vernon & Pittsburg Railroad.

When General Schofield's 23rd Corps was moved by rail from Tennessee to North Carolina in February of 1865 to meet General Sherman's advancing forces, two of the locomotives of the Cleveland, Columbus & Cincinnati were borrowed to aid in the movement of these troops over the Central Ohio Railroad.

SORROWFUL OCCASION

The NASHVILLE of the Cleveland, Columbus & Cincinnati Railroad stands in front of the wooden frame station, ready to handle the Lincoln funeral train. The group of uncovered men ranged around the old Cuyahoga eight-wheeler are probably the operating officials of the road.

(Courtesy of the Library of Congress)

FUNERAL COACH CLOSE-UP

This view shows the car which carried President Lincoln's remains on the long, sad journey from Washington to Springfield. It is coupled into the funeral special operated over the Pennsylvania Railroad; in the background is the crepe-decorated Harrisburg Station and a tank switch engine, No. 328. The honor guard is in position on the car platforms and spectators crowd the balcony of the station.

(Courtesy of the Pennsylvania Railroad)

(Courtesy of the Illinois Central Railroad)

LAST LEG OF A SAD JOURNEY

After the remains of the assassinated President Lincoln had been on display to crowds of mourners in the Court House on Chicago's Clark Street from around noon of May 1st until about 8:00 P.M. of May 2nd, 1865, the casket was removed to the depot of the Chicago, Alton & St. Louis Railroad on Canal Street.

With muffled tolling of bells, the funeral special slowly departed over the Chicago, Alton & St. Louis tracks at 9:30 P.M., headed for the final destination at Springfield, Illinois. The Alton road, later to become part of the Gulf, Mobile & Ohio, was scheduled to deliver the funeral train into Springfield at 6:30 A.M. on May 3rd, but delays en route caused the special to pull into the Springfield station at 9:00 A.M., two and one-half hours late.

The casket was removed from its car and carried to the hall of the House of Representatives in the State House, followed by crowds of mourners; many of them were acquaintances who had known Lincoln personally when he had resided in the city.

On May 4th the earthly remains of the Great Emancipator were conveyed to Springfield's Oak Ridge Cemetery and placed in a vault for temporary interment. At a later date they were again moved, this time to the elaborate combined tomb and monument erected by the State of Illinois.

Since Abraham Lincoln had long been an ardent supporter of American railroads and a moving force in the efforts to span the continent with rails, it was only fitting that his last journey home was behind the Iron Horse.

This photograph shows the Lincoln funeral train moving across a trestle on the Lake Michigan waterfront in Chicago.

The Lincoln funeral train from Chicago to Springfield is reported to have included George M. Pullman's first sleeping car, the PIONEER, added to the train's consist at the request of Mary Todd Lincoln, the President's widow. The PIONEER, built in 1864 at a cost of about $20,000, was too wide for existing clearances and hasty alterations had to be made to station platforms en route to permit it to pass.

The grief of the nation was expressed during the long trip from Washington to Springfield. Bonfires burned along the tracks at night, flagmen protected road crossings, cannon boomed their solemn requiem, and bells tolled their dirges as the funeral train crawled across the land under arches of crepe-hung evergreens. At every major stop where Lincoln's body was displayed, eulogies were offered and crowds jammed the streets for a final look at the great man who had stood at the country's helm through the bitter years of the Civil War, only to be felled by the bullet of John Wilkes Booth as the thunder of battle died away and the task of reconciliation needed his guiding spirit.